SEVEN STEPS

to a

BETTER YOU

*How to develop your
natural tendencies*

JOHN T. COCORIS, TH.M, PSY.D.

7 Steps To A Better You: How To Develop Your Natural Tendencies
©2016 By Dr. John T. Cocoris

johncocoris@sbcglobal.net
www.fourtemperaments.com

ISBN 978-0-9721650-3-7

Profile Dynamics
McKinney, Texas 75070

Cover and interior design by April Beltran
Cover photograph by Zak Suhar

ACKNOWLEDGMENTS

I am indebted to my wife, Darrellene, who shares my vision for this work. We have spent countless hours talking about observations we have both made. She has read and reread the manuscript making helpful suggestions. I am indebted to my brother, Mike, for his guidance and support. He has made valuable contributions to this work. Special thanks to Gary Fusco who edited the manuscript. He shares my passion for using the temperament concept in counseling. Thanks also to Lane Hedgepeth for reading and editing the manuscript. Special thanks to April Beltran who read and edited the manuscript offering insightful suggestions that have made this work better. April is also responsible for the interior layout and the book cover design.

Table of Contents
WHAT YOU'LL DISCOVER INSIDE

INTRODUCTION..1

Chapter One
THE TEMPERAMENT CONCEPT.............................5

Chapter Two
FUNDAMENTAL CONCEPTS....................................9

Chapter Three
FREQUENTLY ASKED QUESTIONS.........................13

Chapter Four
TEMPERAMENT OVERVIEW....................................17

Chapter Five
STEP 1: SELF AWARENESS......................................23

Chapter Six
STEP 2: SELF ACCEPTANCE....................................69

Chapter Seven
STEP 3: SELF EXPRESSION......................................75

Chapter Eight
STEP 4: SELF CONTROL..79

Chapter Nine
STEP 5: BALANCE..101

Chapter Ten
STEP 6: APPRECIATE..107

Chapter Eleven
STEP 7: MODIFY..111

CONCLUSION..117

Introduction

"I WAS DIFFERENT AND I THOUGHT THAT WAS A BAD THING"

I grew up thinking something was wrong with me--I analyzed everything, I did nothing without first planning, and I enjoyed being by myself. I was different, and I thought that was a bad thing. At least, I was different from my brother. My brother Mike was outgoing, impulsive and very talkative. He liked being with people, and he was on the go all the time.

I married at age nineteen still thinking I was deficient in something. Initially, I was attracted to her because she was like my brother...outgoing, spontaneous and she laughed a lot. I thought this would make up for whatever I was missing.

Many years passed, and I found out that I was born with natural tendencies that happened to be different from my brother's natural tendencies. To my amazement, I discovered that I *was* different and different wasn't bad, it was *just* different. I had natural tendencies, and that was the reason I behaved the way I did--at least for the most part. After thinking about it for some time, I decided that I was normal! I decided that my brother was normal too, we were just different.

This is a simple but important truth. People are different because they possess different, natural tendencies called temperament. The word temperament is a very old term that refers to a person's natural disposition. It recognizes that people are born with natural tendencies such as being assertive, friendly, passive, or analytical. According to this position, these traits are enduring and last throughout the lifespan of the individual.

The importance of this concept cannot be overestimated. Many people go through life comparing themselves to another person and almost always come up short. Sometimes people compare themselves to others and decide that the other person has a problem. I was in a bank waiting for a teller to handle my transaction when I heard quite a commotion. I looked over to my right to see an older gentleman (loosely used) leaning over the counter and into the face of the young teller. He was speaking so loud that everyone in the bank could hear him say, "Smile honey, smile!" He repeated it twice and ended with, "Come on honey, smile, it won't hurt!" The poor girl looked like she was about to cry.

Now here was a clear example of a person thinking his approach to life was far better than hers. It was not acceptable to him that she was different, and his tactic was to embarrass her to conform to his standard. She was not like him nor did she need to be. One of him in this world was enough.

Perhaps you are not comfortable with your natural tendencies. Perhaps you have compared yourself to others, and you came up short. Perhaps you think you are a little bit different from others and have decided that is a bad thing. Maybe it's the reverse. Perhaps you think others should be like you. In either case, you need to understand that people are different and different isn't bad.

After introducing him to the temperament concept of human behavior, a psychologist friend of mine told me this story. He had a son that he considered a delight. When he was a baby, he would hold him, and they would "goo" at each other and then laugh and smile. He said, "Wow, being a dad is fun!" Then he had a second son. He thought *"goo-ing" worked the first time, it should also work on the second one.* He went "goo" at him and his second son just looked at him as if to say, "Is that the best you have to offer?" His two sons were different and he was confused. After explaining the temperaments, he understood why this happened.

There have been several books written over the past fifty years about temperament. In those early years, I read what I could find but mainly I talked to people. I started in the early1970's and discovered that nothing had been written about what to do once you knew your temperament blend.

Over the years, I found a natural progression to develop my own natural tendencies. It was the result of my unyielding attempt to make sense out of what difference it meant to know my temperament. I knew my blend but so what? While on my journey, the seven steps started to unfold. As I began living out each new step, it became clear to me that I was becoming a more mature and well-rounded person because of my study and application of the temperament concept.

The seven steps in this book are the results of years of study and personal application of the temperament concept. My hope is that you will follow these steps to help you become a better you.

John T. Cocoris
McKinney, Texas

NOTE

I have written a series of books and manuals on the subject of temperament, and each work represents a different application of the concept. To adequately understand each application, it was necessary to include in each work a variation of the history of the temperament concept, foundational concepts, and common questions.

If this is the only book you read on the subject of the temperaments, then you would need the information in the first few chapters. The material found in the first five chapters of this work is also found in more detail in my book, *The Temperament Model of Behavior: Born With Natural Tendencies.*

Chapter One

THE TEMPERAMENT CONCEPT

The concept of the four temperaments has been around for thousands of years. Simply put, people are born with natural tendencies that can be grouped into four categories. The most archaic terms used are Choleric, Sanguine, Phlegmatic, and Melancholy. The most popular terms used today are High "D" (Dominant), High "I" (Influencing), High "S" (Steadiness), and High "C" (Compliance). The correlations of the terms are Choleric (D), Sanguine (I), Phlegmatic (S), and Melancholy (C).

According to the temperament model of behavior, every person has all four tendencies to some degree, but one of the four has a greater influence than the other three. The primary tendency has the main influence on a person's behavior while another tendency has a secondary influence and so forth. It is the combination of the top two tendencies which produce a blend that urges a person to consistently behave in a particular manner.

In the last half of the twentieth century, there has been a revival of interest in the four temperament concept in the United States. The early writers were focused only on a person's primary temperament. The focus of this work is not just the primary temperament, but the combination of the two strongest tendencies. Considering the temperament *blend* of a person versus only thinking in terms of the primary temperament is like putting a fuzzy picture in focus. In dealing with the temperament concept, it is essential to deal with the blend of the first two temperaments.

The overview chart (see Figure 1) shows various names used to refer to the temperaments. Many more have been used, but these seem to be the most popular ones. The chart also shows the kind of outlook each temperament has on life.

FIGURE 1 | THE FOUR PRIMARY TEMPERAMENT CHART

EXTROVERTS

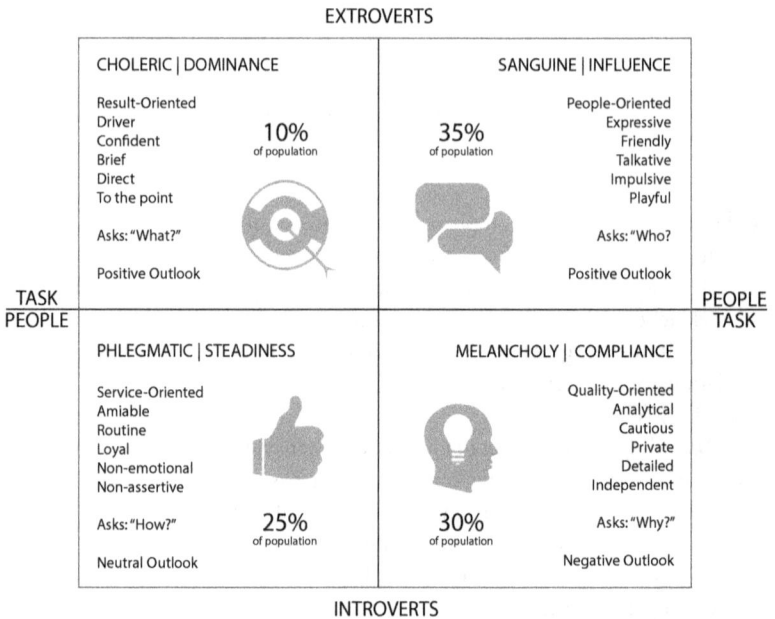

CHOLERIC | DOMINANCE		SANGUINE | INFLUENCE
Result-Oriented Driver Confident **10%** of population Brief Direct To the point		People-Oriented Expressive **35%** of population Friendly Talkative Impulsive Playful
Asks: "What?"		Asks: "Who?
Positive Outlook		Positive Outlook

TASK   PEOPLE
PEOPLE   TASK

PHLEGMATIC | STEADINESS		MELANCHOLY | COMPLIANCE
Service-Oriented Amiable Routine Loyal Non-emotional Non-assertive		Quality-Oriented Analytical Cautious Private Detailed Independent
Asks: "How?" **25%** of population	**30%** of population	Asks: "Why?"
Neutral Outlook		Negative Outlook

INTROVERTS

HISTORICAL OVERVIEW

HIPPOCRATES (C. 460-377 B.C.)

Hippocrates is given credit for observing that people have natural tendencies (temperament). He taught that behavior was determined by the presence of an excessive amount of one of four fluids or humors: yellow bile (Chlor), red bile or blood (Sangis), white bile (Phlegm) or black bile (Melan). By isolating these four fluids he was trying to establish that behavior has a medical origin.

GALEN (AD 129-200 OR 216)

Galen was a Greek physician who lived 600 years after Hippocrates. He related the four temperaments to illness. He is credited with coining the terms Choleric, Sanguine, Phlegmatic, and Melancholy in his dissertation *De temperamentis*.

NICHOLAS CULPEPER (1616-1654)

Nicholas Culpeper was an English botanist, herbalist, physician, and astrologer. He rejected the idea that the four humors were the cause of a person's temperament. He also was the first to say that a person is influenced by two temperaments, one primary and one secondary. Before Culpeper, it was believed that a person was influenced by only one temperament.

IMMANUEL KANT (1724-1804)

Immanuel Kant, a German philosopher, described the temperaments in his book, *Anthropology from a Pragmatic Point of View* (1798). He wrote a description of the four temperaments that was clear and accurate.

CARL JUNG (1875-1961)

Carl Jung, a Swiss psychiatrist, published *Psychological Types* in 1921. The premise of his work was to determine how people take in information and make decisions. Jung coined the terms *extrovert* and *introvert* suggesting that everyone falls into one of the two categories. The extrovert prefers the outer, objective world of things, people, and actions; and the introvert prefers the inner, subjective world of thoughts, ideas, and emotions.

WILLIAM M. MARSTON (1893-1947)

William M. Marston was the first to contribute scientific evidence that people fit into one of four categories. He published his book, *Emotions of Normal People* in 1928 using the terms Dominant, Influence, Steadiness, and Compliance.

OLE HALLESBY (1879-1961)

Ole Hallesby, a Lutheran theology professor in Norway, contributed penetrating insight into temperament behavior. In his book *Temperament and the Christian Faith*, written in the 1930's, he used the terms Choleric, Sanguine, Phlegmatic, and Melancholy.

ISABEL MYERS (1897-1980) & KATHARINE BRIGGS (1875-1968)

Isabel Myers and her mother, Katheryn Briggs, wrote a paper in 1958 titled Myers-Briggs Type Indicator (MBTI) in which they proposed that there are sixteen different personality types. Their work was based on Carl Jung's writings on psychological types.

TIM LAHAYE (1926-   )

Tim LaHaye was the first to popularize the temperament concept within the Christian community. Dr. LaHaye published the first of several books in the 1960's using the terms Choleric, Sanguine, Phlegmatic, and Melancholy. He was the first to write in detail about the dynamics of the temperament blends.

JOHN G. GEIER (1934-2009)

John G. Geier built on the previous works of William M. Marston (1928), Walter Clarke (1940) and John Cleaver (1950). John Geier coined the terms High "D" (Dominant), High "I" (Influencing), High "S" (Steadiness), and High "C" (Competent).

OTHERS

Others have contributed to the temperament model of behavior; Plato (350 BC), Paracelsus (1530), Adickes (1905), Spranger (1914), Kretschmer (1930), Adler (1937), Fromm (1947), Eysenck (1951), and Keirsey (1970).

Chapter Two

FUNDAMENTAL CONCEPTS

The temperament model of behavior is based on several fundamental concepts. Understanding these concepts is essential to correctly applying the temperament model to behavior.

1. EVERYONE HAS TRAITS OF ALL FOUR TEMPERAMENTS

No one is entirely deficient in any one of the temperaments. This allows an individual to demonstrate the traits of any of the four temperaments when the need arises. It is sufficient to know your primary and secondary temperaments, which create the greatest influence on behavior. There are, however, important influences coming from the alignment of the third and fourth temperaments. It is beyond the scope of this work to investigate the impact of such alignments. More information on these alignments can be found in *The DISC II Temperament Assessment: User Guide* (1988), by John T. Cocoris.

2. EACH PERSON HAS A BLEND OF A PRIMARY AND SECONDARY TEMPERAMENT

Everyone has traits of all four temperaments, but all four are not present with equal influence on behavior. The primary temperament will have a stronger influence on behavior than the other three. Of the remaining three, the secondary temperament will have a stronger influence on behavior than the remaining two. The second temperament will always modify the tendencies of the primary temperament in some significant way. The blend of the primary and secondary temperaments will represent a person's normal, usual and daily demeanor.

3. EACH TEMPERAMENT HAS NATURAL STRENGTHS AND WEAKNESSES

Each person will naturally excel at certain tasks while being naturally deficient in performing other tasks. For example, the High "I" (Sanguine) works well with people but is usually weak when working with details, whereas the High "C" (Melancholy) works well with details but will shy away from too much involvement with people.

4. STRENGTHS AND WEAKNESSES REPRESENT BOTH TEMPERAMENTS

All twelve blends will combine strengths and weaknesses representing both temperaments. For example, the D-C (Choleric-Melancholy) blend will combine the strengths and weaknesses of both the High "D" (Choleric) and the High "C" (Melancholy). This combination produces a person who gets results with a detailed plan and can be forceful, explosive, and critical, but can also be gentle and sensitive.

5. STRENGTHS AND WEAKNESSES VARY IN DEGREES OF INTENSITY

The *intensity* of traits present has a significant influence on the expression of a person's temperament tendencies. Two people with the same temperament may demonstrate differences in behavior because one is more intense than the other. Intensity levels vary from mild to moderate, to extreme.

6. A STRENGTH OVEREXTENDED BECOMES A WEAKNESS

Any strength that is overextended (used to an extreme) will become a weakness. For example, the High "D" (Choleric) is naturally brief, direct, and to the point in their communication with others but if they are too direct they become blunt and offensive. The High "I" (Sanguine) tends to talk a lot, but if they talk too much, they will annoy others. The High "S" (Phlegmatic) is naturally accommodating but if they are too accommodating others will take advantage of them. The High "C"

(Melancholy) is naturally analytical but if they are too analytical, they will be paralyzed and never get anything done.

7. STRENGTHS CAN BE DEVELOPED AND WEAKNESSES CAN BE OVERCOME

Each person has the choice to develop their natural temperament strengths and overcome their natural temperament weaknesses. Whether or not a strength is developed or a weakness is overcome, and to what degree, depends on the individual's motivation to become a well-balanced person.

8. TEMPERAMENT TENDENCIES ARE DEVELOPED ACCORDING TO A PERSON'S RESPONSE TO THE VARIABLES IN THEIR ENVIRONMENT

Differences in behavior may be explained by an individual's response to the many variables to which a person is exposed to in their environment. A person is always responsible for the choices they make regardless of their environment.

9. TEMPERAMENT IS AN INNER FORCE THAT PUSHES AND PULLS

This principle enables us to understand the dynamics that occur when the various temperaments are combined. All temperament blend combinations experience internal conflict on some level. The nature of the conflict is that two temperaments representing two different and sometimes opposing forces are at work at the same time, essentially *pushing* and *pulling* the person in two different directions. One temperament will *push* on the individual to act, and at the same time, the other will *pull* the individual back from acting. This produces internal tension. For most of the blends, the internal conflict or tension is not a major issue. There are a few of the blends, however, where the push/pull causes a more serious level of internal conflict and tension.

For most of the blends, the internal conflict or tension is not a major issue. There are a few of the blends, however, where the push/pull causes a more serious level of internal conflict and tension. For example: the D-C (Choleric-Melancholy) blend produces some tension because there is an urgent need to get results conflicting with the need to get right results; the combination of the I-C (Sanguine-Melancholy) blend produces tension because there is a need to be with people conflicting with the need to be alone; and the combination of the C-D (Melancholy-Choleric) blend produces tension because there is need to get right results and the High "C" (Melancholy) will resist being pushed to get results quickly.

Chapter Three

FREQUENTLY ASKED QUESTIONS

WHAT IS TEMPERAMENT?

Temperament represents the way a person relates to others and responds to events. It is what you have observed and expect someone's behavior to be, most of the time. Have you ever referred to someone as shy or outgoing? Without realizing it, you were referring to certain temperament traits. These traits are what you know and expect the person to be every time you are with them.

The four temperaments are represented by four distinct groups of traits or tendencies. Each cluster of traits produces a distinct manner of behavior that is different from the other groups. For example, the High "D" (Choleric) is result-oriented, the High "I" (Sanguine) is people-oriented, the High "S" (Phlegmatic) is service-oriented, and the High "C" (Melancholy) is quality-oriented. Thus, temperament behavior is, for the most part, predictable. The exception being when one temporarily experiences strong emotions, such as anger or fear, or is trying to deceive another. Actually, acting is a form of acceptable deception. A person is knowingly acting like they are someone else. Unfortunately, some purposely act like someone they are not in order to deceive.

Because someone's temperament is inborn, it is a force which pushes or urges you to behave according to the tendencies that represent your temperament blend. You can also think of temperament as a need. Abraham Maslow says that a need is something that if you do not meet, you become sick. Air, food, and water are physical needs without which a person would become ill and die. If your temperament needs are not met, you will not die, but you will become emotionally and eventually physically ill. Stress-related illness is often the result of a temperament need not being met. Meeting temperament needs is critical to a person's sense of well-being and feeling of self-worth.

WHAT TEMPERAMENT IS NOT

Many people often confuse temperament with character, personality or type. First of all, temperament has nothing to do with a person's character or their level of maturity. Character reflects the choices that are made. A person's temperament is also not the same as their personality. There are many factors that make up the total personality of a person—temperament is only one part. Lastly, temperament is not a type. Types are broad categories such as extrovert or introvert. Someone's temperament, as mentioned in the section above, is composed of traits. While types are broad categories, traits are more narrow and specific characteristics of behavior such as being direct, sociable, patient, or analytical.

NOTE: The temperament model does not embrace the type approach to behavior. Rather, the temperament model recognizes that people are born with a cluster of traits which allows for different degrees of expression or development by an individual. Gordon Allport says, "A man can be said to have a trait, but he cannot be said to have a type, rather he fits a type."

WHAT IS THE ORIGIN OF TEMPERAMENT?

There are two possibilities: either people are *born without* natural tendencies, or they are *born with* natural tendencies. Some believe that people start life with a blank slate (referred to as tabula rasa) and that the environment determines the personality as individuals have exchanges with their surroundings. Others teach that a person is born with natural tendencies and that these traits are developed according to that person's *response* to their environment.

The temperament model of behavior teaches that people are born with various *traits*. If you want proof that children are born with natural tendencies, just ask a mother who has raised at least two children. She will tell you that they were different from birth. My daughter has twin girls and knew before they were born that one was going to be very active, and the other one was going to be more gentle, and that is exactly how they are today.

WILL MY TEMPERAMENT BLEND EVER CHANGE?

No. The temperament blend that you were born with remains throughout your lifespan. Some think that because they have experienced some growth, their temperament blend has somehow changed. All that has happened is that they have learned self-control and have matured.

CAN ANYONE BE A LEADER OR MANAGER REGARDLESS OF THEIR TEMPERAMENT?

Yes. A person will lead based on their temperament. The High "D" (Choleric) and High "I" (Sanguine) will lead by directing. They will tell you to get a task completed. The High "S" (Phlegmatic) and High "C" (Melancholy) will lead by example. They will show you how to complete the task. Each one will be effective in their own way. Consider the following Presidents of the United States: Lyndon Johnson, High "D"; Ronald Reagan, High "I"; Gerald Ford, High "S"; George W. Bush, High "C."

Chapter Four

TEMPERAMENT OVERVIEW

THE FOUR PRIMARY TEMPERAMENTS

As has been pointed out, there are four primary temperaments. The first two are *extroverts,* and the other two are *introverts.* Extroverts are active and process oriented. From their point of view, the environment is made to provide the satisfaction that they want. Introverts tend to be passive, private and accommodating. They tend to adapt to whatever the environment has to offer. They are production oriented. Here is a brief explanation of the four primary temperaments:

THE HIGH "D" (CHOLERIC) | The High "D" is extroverted, hot-tempered, quick thinking, active, practical, strong-willed, easily annoyed and result-oriented. The High "D" has a huge ego, a firm expression, and is self-confident, self-sufficient and very independent minded. They are decisive, opinionated and find it easy to make decisions for themselves as well as others.

THE HIGH "I" (SANGUINE) | The High "I" is extroverted, impulsive, fun-loving, activity-prone, entertaining, persuasive, easily amused, optimistic and people-oriented. The High "I" tends to be competitive, impulsive and disorganized. The voice of the High "I" will show excitement and friendliness. They have a natural smile and talk easily and often. They are animated, excitable and accepting of others. They build relationships quickly and have lots of friends.

THE HIGH "S" (PHLEGMATIC) | The High "S" is introverted, calm, unemotional, slow moving, easygoing, accommodating and service-oriented. The High "S" does not show much emotion and will have a stoic expression. They are slow to warm up and indirect when interacting with others. The High "S" lives a quiet, peaceful, routine life, free of the normal anxieties of the other temperaments. They avoid getting too involved with people and life.

THE HIGH "C" (MELANCHOLY) | The High "C" is introverted, logical, analytical, factual, private, conscientious, timid and quality-oriented. The High "C" will (most always) have a serious expression. They usually respond to others in a slow, cautious and indirect manner. They are self-sacrificing, creative and can be perfectionists. The High "C" has high standards to avoid mistakes.

THE TWELVE TEMPERAMENT BLENDS

Blends with the same primary temperament will have many tendencies in common as well as many tendencies that differ due to the influence of the second temperament. For a more in-depth treatment see *The Temperament Model of Behavior: Born With Natural Tendencies*, by John T. Cocoris.

THREE HIGH "D" (CHOLERIC) BLENDS

D-I *(Choleric-Sanguine)*
This blend is more people-oriented than the other High "D." People with this blend are so result-oriented that they often run over others to get what they want. They easily intimidate others because of their confidence and direct method of communicating.

D-S *(Choleric-Phlegmatic)*
This blend is more determined, unemotional and individualistic than the other High "D." People with this blend tend to be very cold and unresponsive to the emotional needs of others. They are very practical and "down-to-earth."

D-C *(Choleric-Melancholy)*
This blend is more detail-oriented than the other High "D." People with this blend can be both cold and uncaring, or gracious and sensitive. They usually operate from a well-thought through plan. They have creative ideas and initiate change. They have command in their voice. Children are attracted to their confidence.

THREE HIGH "I" (SANGUINE) BLENDS

I-D *(Sanguine-Choleric)*
This blend is more assertive than the other High "I." They are energetic, positive, and work well with and through people. They tend to be confident in their abilities, and they like to lead others.

They easily and naturally influence others. They have an outgoing interest in people and have the ability to gain respect and confidence from others. People with this blend try to persuade others to their point of view.

I-S *(Sanguine-Phlegmatic)*
This blend is more relationship-oriented than the other High "I." They are very approachable and place high importance on enduring relationships. They impress others with their warmth, empathy, and understanding approach. They possess a casual kind of poise in social situations. Children like them and people tend to seek them out to tell them their problems. They are well balanced and stable.

I-C *(Sanguine-Melancholy)*
This blend is more formal than the other High "I." They are sensitive, emotional and creative. They tend to be very concerned about making a favorable impression. They function best when they have a detailed plan, social contact and time alone to think and plan. They are moody and are capable of sudden shifts in their emotions.

THREE HIGH "S" (PHLEGMATIC) BLENDS

S-D *(Phlegmatic-Choleric)*
This blend is more industrious, determined, rigid, and unemotional than the other High "S." This persistent individual brings a deceptively intense approach to their work. Being low-key outwardly—their commitment to a task is not easily observed. People with this blend tend to be more emotionally cold and forcefully resist changing their routine.

S-I *(Phlegmatic-Sanguine)*
This blend is more friendly than the other High "S" combinations. People with this blend tend to be too accommodating to the needs of

others to the point of self-neglect. They want others to know that they have a deep desire to be of help before they can function effectively. They can be very talkative at times.

S-C *(Phlegmatic-Melancholy)*
This blend is more consistent than the other High "S." They are routine, accommodating and passive. Patience, control, and deliberateness characterize the usual behavior of this amiable and easy going individual.

They tend to worry and are very possessive of their possessions, their children, and relationships. Activity tends to center around their home and family. They are very dependable and like to do one thing at a time.

THREE HIGH "C" (MELANCHOLY) BLENDS

C-D *(Melancholy-Choleric)*
This blend is more precise and picky than the other High "C" blends. Because of the secondary "D" tendencies, they push their view as the right way. They are very attentive to detail and push to have things done correctly according to their standards. They are extremely conscientious and painstaking in work requiring accuracy and maintaining standards. They can be a perfectionist. At times, they can be abrupt and abrasive.

C-I *(Melancholy-Sanguine)*
This blend is more friendly than the other High "C" blends. They have high personal ambitions. This is a well-balanced, systematic, precise thinker who tends to follow procedures in both their business and personal life. Their activity centers around their family or people with whom they are comfortable. They can be very talkative at times.

C-S *(Melancholy-Phlegmatic)*
This blend is more conscientious and private than the other High "C" blends. This quiet individual works well in a structured environment requiring attention to detail. They make decisions slowly because of collecting and analyzing information until they are sure of the right and the best course of action (this is especially true when involved in a new project). They need feedback and reassurance that they have made the right decision.

INTERNAL TENSION

As mentioned earlier, all temperament blend combinations experience internal tension on some level. For most of the blends, the internal tension is not a major problem. There are a few of the blends, however, who experience a more serious level of internal tension. The nature of the tension is that two temperaments representing two *different* and *opposing* forces are at work at the same time essentially pulling the person in two different directions causing tension.

THE HIGH "D" (CHOLERIC) BLENDS

A combination of "D-I" (Choleric-Sanguine) or "D-S" (Choleric-Phlegmatic) tendencies do not produce significant internal conflict. The "D-I" (Choleric-Sanguine) tendencies are both extroverted and active. There is also not much conflict when the "D-S" temperament because the secondary "S" is passive and offers no resistance to the primary "D" tendencies (other than slowing him/her down a little).

Internal conflict is observed when the "D-C" (Choleric-Melancholy) are blended together. The primary "D" wants to act first and the secondary "C" wants to plan first. Both tendencies are focused on accomplishing the task. The primary "D" side, however, wants the results quickly, and the secondary "C" portion wants the right results.

If the individual learns to control both so that they plan first and then act, the internal conflict is greatly reduced and this person will become extremely focused and productive. When this is not managed well, there is instability and frequent outbursts of anger.

THE HIGH "I" (SANGUINE) BLENDS

As with the High "D" blends, the same approach applies to the High "I" blends. Not much conflict is observed when the "I-D" (Sanguine-Choleric) are blended because both are extroverted and active. The "I-S" (Sanguine-Phlegmatic) in combination produces very little conflict. However, great internal conflict always occurs when the primary "I" and secondary "C" are in combination.

THE HIGH "S" (PHLEGMATIC) BLENDS

When the High "S" is first in combination with the other three there is generally not much internal conflict. The High "S" tendency has a calming effect on the other temperaments. There is much more internal conflict, however, when the primary "S" is in combination with the secondary "D" because the High "S" part will resist the push of the High "D" tendencies. The "S" and "I" temperaments tend to work well together although there is some conflict produced by the push of the "I" part on the tendency of the "S" to move slowly.

THE HIGH "C" (MELANCHOLY) BLENDS

The greatest internal conflict for the High "C" blends comes from the "C-D" (Melancholy-Choleric) combination. The primary temperament "C" wants to think in great detail while the secondary "D" part just wants results now; these two annoy each other and tend to have a war going on all the time. The other two, "C-I" (Melancholy-Sanguine) and the "C-S" (Melancholy-Phlegmatic) tend to work very well together with little internal conflict.

THE GREATEST INTERNAL CONFLICT

The greatest internal conflict occurs when the "I" (Sanguine) is primary and the "C" (Melancholy) is secondary. These two are in opposition to each other in almost every way. The primary "I" part wants to be with people and the secondary "C" part wants to be alone. The "I" side is spontaneous and the "C" portion wants to plan. The "I" part wants to have fun and the "C" part wants to do something serious. The "I" part is disorganized and the "C" part is organized. The "I" part talks all the time and the "C" part speaks when it has something to say.

As you can easily see, these opposites stay at war with each other and often cause great difficulty for people hosting this blend. They are pulled in both, even opposite directions, most of the time. They often tell me they stay confused because they don't know if they should go do something with someone or think first and then make a plan!

NOTE: Those who are familiar with the DISC model will recognize that the letters "I-C" represent Influence (I) and Compliance (C). The "I-C" is the High "I" (Sanguine)-High "C" (Melancholy). The Letters I-C were coined from John Geier's work in the early 1970's. The terms Choleric, Sanguine, Phlegmatic, and Melancholy were coined by Galen sometime around 200 A.D.

It is important to know that the terms Sanguine and Melancholy are deeply rooted in history and not a recent concept.

Chapter Five

STEP ONE: SELF AWARENESS

Discover Your Temperament Blend

The first step to a ***better you*** is to become aware of your natural temperament tendencies.

None of us can remember when we were a baby, but there was a first time when we became aware that we had a hand. Something kept waving in front of our face, and we soon realized that it wasn't going away. Then we found our toes; my mother called them "piggy's," and the first thing we wanted to do with this new found "thing" was put it in our mouth. Somehow it just seemed right. In time we all discovered our nose, eyes, ears, and that we could make noise. As we grew, we became more and more accustomed to out bodies. Some of us accepted what we found and some did not.

As we continued to grow, our bodies not only developed but also our personalities. It takes time to figure out how our body works and what makes us tick, but it takes more time to figure out our personality. How many have asked, *"Why did I do that?"* or, *"Why am I not like my brother or sister?"* As parents of at least two, ever wonder why your children are different? Carl Jung (1875-1961) a Swiss psychiatrist said, *"Your visions will become clear only when you can look into your own heart. Who looks outside...dreams, who looks inside...awakes."*

How important is self-awareness? It is what awakens us to a conscious level of understanding and acceptance of what we might not have known before. At some point during the journey through life, most have said, *"I did not know that about myself."* This may be either a pleasant or unpleasant experience, but it should always result in personal growth.

JOHARI'S WINDOW

A helpful tool that identifies our lack of self-awareness is Johari's Window. This four-paned "window" as shown in Figure 2 divides personal awareness into four different categories. The four panes are like windows representing various levels of self-awareness: the OPEN quadrant represents things that both I know about

myself and you know about me; the BLIND quadrant represents things that you
know about me, but I am unaware of; the HIDDEN quadrant represents things
I know about myself that you do not know; the UNKNOWN quadrant represents
things that neither I know about myself, nor you know about me.

Johari's Window teaches that there are things about ourselves that we may
not be aware of called blind spots. Before anyone can gain control over the things
that may be interfering with their life, they must first become aware of their
behavior.

FIGURE 2 | JOHARI'S WINDOW

Known to Self OPEN Known to Others	Unknown to Self BLIND Known to Others
Known to Self HIDDEN Unknown to Others	Unknown to Self UNKNOWN Unknown to others

JOHARI'S WINDOW APPLIED

Johari's window is a key concept that will guide you toward maximizing your
potential. Notice the four window panes:

Open
The goal is to become a more congruent person. To be congruent
means that what people see on the outside represents what you are on
the inside. When you are open, you are perceived to be a genuine,

authentic person that does not change if the circumstances are different. For example, you are the same at a social gathering as you are at home with your family.

Blind

There are some things about yourself that you may not see. To achieve more congruence, you need to increase your self-awareness by knowing your temperament strengths and weaknesses. For example, you may talk too loud around others and not be aware of what you are doing. Be open as you read about your natural tendencies in the next chapter; it may reveal some blind spots. Once understood, choose to make the necessary corrections.

Hidden

There may be some things that you are concealing from others which hinder you from becoming a more congruent person. For example, you may secretly want to play a musical instrument, but you keep it to yourself due to a fear of what others might think. There may be some things you would like to try, but you are afraid of failing. Be willing to investigate what you may be hiding from others out of fear.

Unknown

There are things that you do not know about *yourself* and others do not know about you. Be open as you investigate what it means to be your temperament. You may be pleasantly surprised at what you discover about yourself.

TEMPERAMENT AND SELF-AWARENESS

A major benefit of knowing your temperament blend is that it will increase your *self-awareness*. You will become more aware of your natural strengths and natural weaknesses. Once aware, you will be able to use your strengths, and consciously work on overcoming your weaknesses. You will be able to identify specific needs that, when met, will enable you to live a more fulfilling life. Knowing about the temperaments will also help you see why people are different, which will increase your appreciation for a different approach. Everyone has a natural, normal way of approaching people and events based on their temperament blend.

WHAT'S MY TEMPERAMENT BLEND?

To identify your temperament blend, read through the fifteen pattern descriptions in the next chapter. Select the pattern with which you are the most comfortable—the one with which you feel describes you best; at least in 85% agreement. Be able to say, "That's me most of the time." Higher the level of agreement, the better.

Be sure that you pick the one that you are, and not the one that you want to be. Do not force yourself to agree with the blend that you have selected. When you read the blend that describes you, you will recognize that it is mostly accurate and correct. Remember, temperament is what you are **most** of the time, it is your most natural and comfortable way of behaving. Rate your response to each blend on a scale between 1 and 10 as illustrated below:

Like me 10---9---8---7---6---5---4---3---2---1 Not like me

You might have someone who knows you well read the pattern you have selected. Ask if it describes you, and have them rate their response on the same scale as above. The idea is that the individual would agree with your selection and rate it about the same.

HIGH D | CHOLERIC

Primary & temperament blends

DIRECT **DARING** DECISIVE **DETERMINED** DOMINEERING **RISK-TAKER** SELF-RELIANT **FIRM** ASSERTIVE **COMPETITIVE** CONTROLLING **CONFIDENT** BOLD **FEARLESS** IMPATIENT **QUICKLY AROUSED** EASILY CALMED **EASILY BORED** EASILY ANNOYED **LIKES PRESSURE**

The high "D" (Choleric) is naturally result-oriented. They have active, positive and forward movement in an antagonistic environment. They influence their environment by overcoming opposition to get results. The High "D" is the least occurring of the four temperaments, and a female High "D" is very rare. The High "D" temperament has three combinations and four common patterns:

COMBINATION	PATTERN
D-I *(Choleric-Sanguine)*	Executive & Motivator
D-S *(Choleric-Phlegmatic)*	Director
D-C *(Choleric-Melancholy)*	Strategist

The traits of the primary temperament, "D," will be altered or modified in some significant way because of the influence of the secondary temperament. Remember, there are at least three levels of intensity of a temperament: classic, moderate and mild. Some "D" will be very strong, others somewhat strong and still others milder.

Those with a High "D" are extroverted, hot-tempered, quick-thinking, active, practical, strong-willed and easily annoyed. They are self-confident, self-sufficient, and very independent minded. They are brief, direct, to the point and firm when communicating with others. High "D's" like pressure and are easily bored when things are not happening fast enough. They are bold and like to take risks.

High "D's" are domineering, decisive, opinionated, and they find it easy to make decisions for themselves as well as for others. They wake up wanting to control, change or overcome something, anything! They leave little room for negotiating—it's usually their way or no way.

High "D's" are visionaries and seem never to run out of ideas, plans and goals, which are all usually practical. They do not require as much sleep as the other temperaments, so their activity seems endless. Their activity, however, always has a purpose because of their goal-oriented nature.

High "D's" usually do not give in to the pressure of what others think unless they see that they cannot get their desired results. They can be crusaders against social injustice, and they love to fight for a cause. They are slow to build relationships and tend to have only a few close friends because results are more important than people. High "D's" do not easily empathize with the feelings of others or show compassion. They think big and seek positions of authority.

The philosopher Immanuel Kant (1798), in his book, *Anthropology from a Pragmatic Point of View*, states:

> We say of a choleric man he is fiery, burns up quickly like straw-fire, and can be readily appeased if others give in to him; there is no hatred in his anger, and, in fact, he loves someone all the more for promptly giving in to him. In short, the choleric is the least fortunate of all the temperaments, since it is the one that arouses most opposition to itself.

The theologian Ole Hallesby (1962) says this about the High "D" in *Temperament and the Christian Faith*:

> The will is the predominant natural element. It is the will that reacts first to external impressions. What the choleric person experiences leads him at once to some decision and his decisions usually result in action.

A word of caution is necessary. The High "D" temperament is often misunderstood and misapplied to others. Those who know about the four temperaments will say a person is High "D" when they are assertive or direct. Just because someone acts this way does not mean that they are a High "D" by nature. The litmus test is whether or not the High "D" is matter-of-fact, brief, direct and to the point without being offensive. Others who do these things and do not have the High "D" temperament tend to be abrasive and offensive. This will become clearer as you learn about the behavior of the other temperaments.

The following represents High "D's" in general, but individual differences will occur based on the influence of the second temperament. Also, what a person is exposed to from an early age plays a vital role in these areas, but remember an individual is still responsible for the choices they make. Regardless of one's natural tendencies, discipline applied in any area will control and overcome a weakness or extreme behavior. The goal is to become a well-balanced person, being in control of thoughts, feelings and behavior.

D-I BLEND
THE EXECUTIVE
Choleric-Sanguine

The "D-I" (Choleric-Sanguine) blend is expressed in the Executive and Motivator patterns. The Executive pattern has less Sanguine tendencies than the Motivator pattern and is, therefore, more forceful and result-oriented. They expect the environment to adapt to their demands. The Motivator pattern is discussed next. The Executive is one of the least frequently found patterns.

The Executive pattern is driven by two temperament needs. The primary need is to get results. The secondary need is to be accepted socially. Either need may dominate their behavior depending on the requirements of the situation. When the "D" and the "I" natural tendencies are combined in the Executive's blend, it produces a result-oriented person who needs to be around people socially some of the time.

DESCRIPTION

Executives have a natural drive to get results, now. The Executive is quickly aroused emotionally but easily calmed. They are goal and bottom-line oriented and can be very persuasive in promoting their ideas. They are easily annoyed when others do not comply with their instructions or direction, but it passes quickly. They are not angry, although others may think they are furious. They are impatient and will push others to obtain results and be productive.

They take a win/lose approach to life, so when results are not coming quickly enough, they become bored and will move easily to another project. They have boundless energy and need lots of activity. They require little sleep (4 to 6 hours is common). They dislike details or doing tedious work.

Executives need daily challenges and others willing to listen to them and carry out their plans. This versatile, eager, self-starter is very competitive. They like having power and authority and will actively seek leadership positions. They want to be in charge because of confidence in their ability to make decisions and get results. Executives are very practical and will use direct methods to get results but still show some interest and concern for people. Executives are driven by an active will which is apparent in their unyielding determination to accomplish their goals. Executives will fight for their way in accomplishing a goal, but they can accept momentary defeat, and tend not to be grudge holders. They dislike weakness in those with whom they are associated.

They need some social involvement but not much. They have a high drive to win, work, and control people and events. They have a firm expression, a penetrating stare and may appear arrogant.

STRENGTHS

The Executive is naturally result-oriented. They speak with confidence, and they are direct when expressing their thoughts and feelings—you never have to wonder what they are thinking! They have a drive to get results quickly and move to another project. They are decisive and have good social skills which they use effectively to influence others to get results. They are self-motivated and tend to be a practical problem solver.

WEAKNESSES

The Executive's effectiveness in relationships and productivity in their career are often hindered because of their impatience and lack of empathy. They are easily annoyed and will try to control and dominate others and events. They can be abrupt, blunt and explosive. They tend to lack compassion. They are vulnerable to others that can help them get quicker results. They do not seem to realize (or care) that they push people too hard to get results.

NEEDS

The Executive will perform at their best and be highly motivated if their natural, basic needs are met, such as: having the possibility of getting results quickly, having the freedom to control their schedule, having the opportunity for advancements, having difficult assignments and personal challenges with activity, and the freedom from details. The Executive needs the results to come quickly, or they will get bored and move to another project. They also need someone else to give them information that will help them get results (they prefer not to do the research). They need positions of authority due to their high ego strength.

D-I BLEND
THE MOTIVATOR
Choleric-Sanguine

The "D-I" (Choleric-Sanguine) blend is expressed in the Executive and Motivator patterns as previously mentioned. The Motivator pattern is driven by two temperament needs. The primary need is to get results. The secondary need is to be accepted socially. Either need may dominate their behavior depending on the requirements of the situation. When the "D" and the "I" natural tendencies are combined in the Motivator's blend, it produces a result-oriented person who values relationships.

The Motivator pattern has more Sanguine tendencies than the Executive pattern and is, therefore, more charming and inspirational. This is the major difference in these two patterns. The Motivator pattern is one of the least found in society.

DESCRIPTION

Motivators have a natural, strong confidence in their ability to influence people and get results quickly. They have a firm but lively expression. They have a high drive to win, work and control people and events. They tend to be egotistical, enthusiastic and very energetic. They like having power and authority. The Motivator is quickly aroused emotionally but easily calmed--especially after others give in to their demands. They can be very charming. They easily and naturally influence and inspire others to take action. They easily convince others to their point of view. They are quickly annoyed when others do not comply with their instruction or direction.

They are usually practical and use direct methods to get results quickly while maintaining relationships with people. They are goal and bottom-line oriented and can be very forceful in promoting their ideas. They tend to be very impatient and will often take a win/lose approach to life.

They want to be in charge because of confidence in their ability to make better decisions. Motivators have boundless energy and need activity, and quick results, or they will become bored. This versatile, eager self-starter is very competitive.

They need daily, personal challenges and others willing to listen to them to carry out their plans. They dislike a show of weakness in others.

Motivators fight for what they think is the right way to accomplish a goal, but they can accept momentary defeat and tend not to be grudge holders. They need social involvement and use their social contacts to promote themselves. They may change careers often. If results are not coming quickly, they will move to another project. They require little sleep, having only five to six hours is not unusual. They dislike details, doing research and doing tedious work.

STRENGTHS

The Motivator easily influences and inspires others to take action. They are highly motivated to get results quickly to move on to another project. They thrive on social influence and believe that they can motivate others better than anyone else. They are decisive and confident in everything they do.

WEAKNESSES

The Motivator's effectiveness in relationships and productivity in their career is often hindered because of their impatience and explosiveness. They are easily annoyed and can be very abrupt and blunt, alienating others in the process. They often lack follow-through. They are vulnerable to others who can help them get quicker results.

NEEDS

The Motivator will perform at their best and be self-motivated if their natural, basic needs are met such as the possibility of quick results, having difficult assignments, personal challenges, activity, and freedom from meticulous details. They need personal involvement with others. They need, and will seek, positions of authority and influence due to their high ego strength. It is important to the Motivator that they are involved with a team. They tend to frustrate others because of pushing them to get more results.

D-S BLEND
THE DIRECTOR
Choleric-Sanguine

The High "D-S" (Choleric-Phlegmatic) blend is driven by two temperament needs. Their primary need is to get results. Their secondary need is to accommodate others. Either need may dominate their behavior depending on the requirements of the situation. When the "D" and the "S" natural tendencies are combined in the Director's blend, it produces a result-oriented person who is unemotional and unyielding when attempting to accomplish a goal.

The Director is more individualistic and unyielding than the other High "D" patterns. The Director is one of the least frequently found patterns.

DESCRIPTION

The Director is naturally a result-oriented, determined, unemotional and focused individual. The Director has a strong, stubborn will. They are independent and individualistic. They have a firm, stoic expression (flat affect) on their face, and they rarely smile. They are not open, friendly, animated or talkative. They slowly build a few close relationships and will help only those they consider to be their friend.

They are confident and may appear aloof. They want to be in charge because of confidence in their ability to make better decisions. They can be very direct, brief and blunt when answering questions. They tend to be impatient, especially when instructing others. They dislike weakness in others.

They are very practical and will use direct and persistent methods to get results or promote their ideas. Directors can be very blunt and sarcastic when annoyed. They can be very stubborn and resistant to change due to their ability to focus on accomplishing a task. They exhibit an unyielding determination to follow their routine. They are very focused and can bowl over others when pursuing a goal, without showing much concern.

Directors need to know the big picture and have clear, concrete directions before they can function efficiently. They tend to have difficulty working with others because of their independent nature, bluntness and lack of natural people skills.

They will lose interest in a project once the challenge is gone or the results are not coming quickly enough. They usually have deep personal goals and may fail to identify with the company. They often resist being a team member unless the team agrees with their method of achieving a goal. They get drowsy when sitting for only a few minutes and they can go to sleep quickly.

STRENGTHS

The Director has strong self-determination that drives them to be productive in their career. They are unyielding in pursuit of results. They rarely give up once they decide on a goal. They are practical problem solvers. They are direct and confident in their abilities. They are emotionally stable and consistent in everything they do.

WEAKNESSES

The Director's effectiveness in relationships and productivity in their career are often hindered because of being impersonal, unemotional, and blunt. They often lack empathy and compassion and are too impersonal. They can be too independent and seek personal goals instead of company goals. They are easily annoyed and will show a sudden burst of anger when frustrated, but it usually subsides quickly.

They are vulnerable to others that can help them get quicker results. They tend to burn people out by pushing them to get more results quicker. They will often stubbornly resist changing their routine.

NEEDS

The Director will perform at their best and be highly motivated if their natural, basic needs are met, such as the possibility of quick results, the freedom to work alone, difficult assignments, personal challenges and the freedom from too many details (they can handle some details). They have a strong need for independence, activity with routine, the opportunity for advancement, and someone else to give them information that will help them get quicker results. They have a strong need to control their schedule and get results quickly so they can move on to another project. If the results are not coming quickly enough, they lose interest and will look for another project. They need and seek positions of authority due to their high ego strength.

D-C BLEND
THE STRATEGIST
Choleric-Melancholy

The "D-C" (Choleric-Melancholy) blend is driven by two needs. Their primary need is to get results. The secondary need is to do things right. Either need may dominate their behavior depending on the requirements of the situation. When the "D" and the "C" tendencies are combined in the Strategist's blend, it produces a result-oriented, detailed person who plans and pushes their way through life. The Strategist will always operate from a well-thought through, detailed plan.

Strategists are more detail-oriented and sensitive than the other High "D" blends. The Strategist is a frequently found pattern.

DESCRIPTION

The Strategist is a result-oriented, detailed person who is not interested in social involvement. They are driven by a strong will to achieve their plan. They can be direct, blunt and forceful, yet at times show great sensitivity. They can be both domineering and compassionate (they can be both a Lion and a Lamb). They are easily annoyed and quickly aroused, but easily calmed down.

They are a creative problem solver who naturally develops strategies to achieve a goal. They function best when they collect facts and have alone time to think and develop a plan of action. In the process of developing their plan, they will ask direct and detailed questions and can be very forceful and blunt. They prefer work to involvement with people. They have confidence in their voice.

Children are easily drawn to them because of their confidence and sensitive side. Children feel secure in their presence. They initiate change and operate from a well-thought-out plan. Strategists will often use very direct, forceful, and persistent methods to get results or promote their ideas. They want to be in charge because of the confidence in their ability to make things happen the right way. Strategists like to solve problems and make decisions and are quite capable of doing so. They usually have clear goals and are very independent in their attempt to carry them out. They need to know what is expected before they can function efficiently.

They speak with authority and are usually very productive in whatever they undertake. When committed to accomplishing a goal, they are insightful and creative. They dislike weakness in others and do not like to repeat what they have said.

STRENGTHS

The Strategist is creative, practical and will operate from a detailed plan to get results. They are direct, and decisive. They respond well to a challenge by developing a detailed strategy to accomplish the objective. They are excellent for developing strategies to solve problems and will get excited about having a problem to analyze and solve. Once the plan is determined, they are very confident in their ability to obtain the desired results. They seek difficult tasks. If they are not involved in a challenging task, they become bored and restless.

WEAKNESSES

The Strategist's effectiveness in relationships and productivity in their career is often hindered because of their impatience and lack of sensitivity, compassion, and empathy. They can be explosive when frustrated by a lack of results. They tend to do crisis communication. They can be moody because they think too much about the wrong thing. They are vulnerable to others who can help them get quicker results. People under them experience burnout because of being pushed to get quicker results. They often have difficulty delegating responsibility because they want to maintain too much control. They have difficulty trusting others.

NEEDS

The Strategist will perform at their best and be highly motivated if their basic, natural needs are met, such as the possibility of quick results, freedom to establish their schedule, information that will help them get quick results and the chance to make something better. They need difficult assignments that require detailed planning. They need activity, challenges, independence, positions of authority and the opportunity for advancement. They need others to carry out their plans. They need, and will seek, positions of authority due to their large ego strength.

HIGH I | SANGUINE

Primary & temperament blends

EMOTIONAL **ENTHUSIASTIC** EXPRESSIVE **ENTERTAINING**
PERSUASIVE**PERSONABLE**POISED**POPULAR**PLAYFUL
ARTICULATE AFFECTIONATE **ANIMATED**APPROACHABLE
TRUSTING LIFE-OF-THE-PARTY **IMPULSIVE** OPTIMISTIC
E F F E R V E S C E N T **TA L K A T I V E** D I S O R G A N I Z E D

Those with the High "I" (Sanguine) temperament are naturally people-oriented. They have an active, positive movement in a favorable environment. They influence their environment by encouraging others to work together. The Sanguine temperament has three combinations and four common patterns that frequently appear:

COMBINATION	PATTERN
I-D *(Sanguine-Choleric)*	Negotiator-Marketer
I-S *(Sanguine-Phlegmatic)*	Relater
I-C *(Sanguine-Melancholy)*	Performer

The traits of the primary temperament, "I", will be altered or modified in some significant way due to the influence of the secondary temperament. Remember, there are at least three levels of intensity of a temperament: classic, moderate, and mild. Some High "I's" will be very strong, others somewhat strong and still others milder.

High "I's"are extroverted, fun-loving, playful, activity-prone, impulsive, entertaining, persuasive, easily amused and optimistic. They are enthusiastic, expressive and tend to be very affectionate. High "I's" are personable, receptive, open to others and build relationships quickly. They are animated, excitable, approachable, accepting and trusting of others. High "I's" are naturally people-oriented. They have an active, positive movement in a favorable environment. They influence their environment by encouraging others to work together. The traits of the primary temperament, Sanguine, will be altered or modified in some significant way due to the influence of the secondary temperament. Remember, there are at least three levels of intensity of a temperament: classic, moderate, and mild. Some High "I's" will be very strong, others somewhat strong and still others milder. Some are "Super High "I's'" because they are so talkative and active that they are overwhelming.

High "I's" are extroverted, fun-loving, playful, activity-prone, impulsive, entertaining, persuasive, easily amused and optimistic. They are enthusiastic, expressive and tend to be very affectionate. High "I's" are personable, receptive, open to others and build relationships quickly. They are animated, excitable, approachable, accepting and trusting of others. They will smile and talk easily and often. High "I's" are wordsmiths.

It is not unusual to feel as if you have known one who is Sanguine for years after the first meeting. They make and keep friends easily. They get so involved in conversations that they easily forget about time and are often late arriving at their destination. High "I's" are easily bored if not involved in social activity. High "I's" dislike solitude. Their attention span is based on whether or not they are interested in the person or event. They can change their focus or interest in an instant if they become bored.

When telling a story, High "I's" often exaggerate what happened or leave out important details. They make the story exciting, and they don't let the facts get in the way!

High "I's" are competitive and tend to be disorganized. They sometimes have difficulty controlling their thoughts and emotions. They tend not to store their thoughts and feelings—if they think it or feel it, they share it! They usually like sports of any kind because of the activity and involvement with people. Their voice will show excitement and friendliness. High "I's" enjoy dressing according to current fashion. They fear rejection or not making a favorable impression. High "I's" also fear others viewing them as unsuccessful. High "I's" are very effective working with others.

The philosopher, Immanuel Kant (1798), in his book, *Anthropology from a Pragmatic Point of View*, says:

> *A sanguine person manifests his way of sensing and can be recognized by the following traits: he is carefree and full of hope; he attaches great importance to each thing for the moment, and the next moment may not give it another thought. He makes promises in all honesty but fails to keep his word because he has not reflected deeply enough beforehand whether he will be able to keep it. He is a good companion and high-spirited, who*

is reluctant to take anything seriously and all men are his friends.

The theologian Ole Hallesby (1962) says this about the High "I" in *Temperament and the Christian Faith*:

> *The sanguine attitude toward one's surroundings is a receptive mood. Impressions from without have easy access to mind and heart. The explanation for this receptivity of spirit lies in the fact that in the sanguine temperament, the feelings are predominant. And it is one's feelings that are most easily stirred by impressions from without.*

The following represents High "I's" in general but individual differences will occur based on the influence of the second temperament. Also, what a person is exposed to from an early age plays a vital role in these areas, but remember an individual is still responsible for the choices they make. Regardless of one's natural tendencies, discipline applied in any area will control and overcome a weakness or extreme behavior. The goal is to become a well-balanced person, being in control of thoughts, feelings and behavior.

I-D BLEND
THE NEGOTIATOR
Sanguine-Choleric

The I-D (Sanguine-Choleric) blend is expressed in the Negotiator and Marketer patterns. The I-D is driven by two temperament needs. The primary need is to be accepted socially. The secondary need is to get results. Either need may dominate their behavior depending on the requirements of the situation.

When the "I" and the "D" natural tendencies are combined in the Negotiator's blend, it produces a people-person who is goal-oriented and pushes their way through life trying to persuade others to their point of view.

The Negotiator pattern has more "D" tendencies and is, therefore, more forceful and result-oriented than the Marketer pattern, which is discussed next. The Negotiator is a somewhat common pattern.

DESCRIPTION

Negotiators are more assertive than the other High "I" blends, and they easily convince others to their point of view. Negotiators are very persuasive and make good debaters! They are very energetic, work well with and through people and make good leaders. They have an outgoing interest in others and the ability to gain the respect and confidence of various types of individuals. They strive to do business in a friendly way while pushing forward to win their objectives. They have a firm, lively and friendly expression.

They can coordinate events and are willing to delegate responsibilities. They exhibit poise and confidence in most situations, especially social events. They will become bored without activity and social involvement.

Negotiators have a difficult time with details, organization, and consistency. They prefer that others give them information that will help them make decisions rather than research it for themselves. They are very optimistic but may not follow through.

The Negotiator has a high need to be with, around, or close to people. They will be active or be with people all the time. While the Negotiator tends to know lots of people, they do not know lots of people *well*--they do not take the time to do so. They are naturally positive, energetic, and enthusiastic about life. They are easily excited, and they have a winsome expression. They can persuade others to their point of view without being offensive. However, they can be egotistical and overbearing at times. They like to tell others what to do and can be too pushy. They live in the present, and they dislike details and structure. They do not plan and will likely "make it up when they wake up!" They often display an attitude that everything they have or do is better. They are competitive. They work in spurts because they like to play. Also, they do not like doing the same thing for very long before they look for something to break the monotony of the moment.

STRENGTHS

The Negotiator temperament has a strong, natural ability to persuade and influence others to their point of view. For this reason, they are regarded as the most powerful of all the temperament blends. They are excellent debaters, salespeople, and natural negotiators. They are friendly, open, sociable, and have contagious enthusiasm. They like a challenge and starting new projects. They are natural leaders--people easily follow them.

WEAKNESSES

The Negotiator's effectiveness in relationships and productivity in their career is often hindered because of a lack of organization, planning, impulsiveness, and they often lack follow-through. They tend to play and talk too much. They can become verbally forceful when communicating their views. They overuse telling others what to do.

NEEDS

The Negotiator will perform at their best and will be highly motivated if their natural, basic needs are met, such as contact with people, acceptance from others, activity, and the opportunity to build social relationships. They have a strong need to be recognized for their accomplishments (this is important to their sense of well-being). They need the freedom to express themselves, to be active, and to have the opportunity to persuade others.

I-D *(sanguine-choleric)* | BURNOUT

The I-D is the only blend that has a tendency to burnout frequently. Both patterns,

Negotiator, and Marketer are affected by this reoccurring event. Typical symptoms of burnout include three to five weeks of excessive activity and displaying intense energy, followed by one to three days of low energy with little or no activity and the need for isolation and rest. The Negotiator uses lots of energy and once their energy level is depleted, rest and down time follows, which allows their body to restore the energy that was used.

To control the effects and reduce the frequency of burnout, the Negotiator should consider reducing their intensity level and taking several five-minute pauses during the day to relax. There are other relaxation techniques that can be practiced daily--do a little research.

If the intensity level can be reduced, you will become more productive. Establish a schedule or routine before the day begins, become more organized, and have a variety of activities instead of one single focus.

I-D BLEND
THE MARKETER
Sanguine-Choleric

The I-D (Sanguine-Choleric) blend is expressed in the Marketer and Negotiator patterns. The I-D is driven by two temperament needs. The primary need is to be accepted socially. The secondary need is to get results. Either need may dominate their behavior depending on the requirements of the situation.

When the "I" and the "D" natural tendencies are combined in the Marketer's blend, it produces a people-person who easily excites others. They have a lively expression, and they will smile easily and laugh often.

The Marketer pattern has less "D" tendencies and is, therefore, more excitable than the Negotiator pattern. The Marketer is a somewhat common pattern.

DESCRIPTION

The Marketer wants to be with people or be active most of the time. They rarely like being alone or inactivity. They are, by far, the most enthusiastic of the other High "I" blends. They can get very excited. These are assertive and energetic people who work well with and through others. They have an outgoing interest in others, and they have the ability to gain the respect and confidence of various types of individuals. They strive to do business in a friendly way while pushing forward to win their objectives. They easily promote their ideas, or the ideas of others. They exhibit poise and confidence in most situations, especially social events. Marketers become bored without activity and social involvement.

They have difficulty with awareness of time, organizing and concentrating on details. They prefer others to give them information that will help them make decisions rather than research it for themselves. They are very optimistic and enthusiastic but lack consistent follow-through. At times, they can display a superior attitude that everything they have and do is better.

The Marketer, like the Negotiator, tends to know lots of people, but they do not know lots of people well--they do not take the time to do so. They get excited about most everything. They have a lively, friendly, open expression and will talk a lot.

Their intensity and acceptance of people naturally elevates the emotional level of others. They can raise the level of emotion just entering a room full of people. They are very active socially, and they like to drop names of people they know.

They have a strong dislike for details and structure but a stronger dislike for routine. They are a "now" person and work in spurts because of their difficulty concentrating on accomplishing one thing at a time. They are easily distracted, disorganized and tend to be inconsistent. They experience emotional burnout often (more at the end of this section). Like the Negotiator pattern, they too will likely "make it up when they wake up!"

STRENGTHS

The Marketer has a natural ability to stir excitement in others. They are full of optimism and enthusiasm. Their contagious emotion naturally lifts the spirits of others just by being in their presence. They are open, sociable and friendly. They naturally develop a large network of people both personally and professionally.

WEAKNESSES

The Marketer's effectiveness in relationships and productivity in their career is often hindered because of a lack of organization and planning. They tend to be inconsistent and lack follow-through. They are impulsive and have a tendency to talk and play too much. They find it difficult to concentrate on doing one thing to completion because they are easily distracted. Their attention span is short. They will overstate and over-promise what they are going to do. They can easily overlook obvious flaws in others because they are so optimistic about people and life in general.

NEEDS

The Marketer will perform at their best and will be highly motivated if their natural, basic needs are met, such as having the freedom to express themselves, a flexible schedule, mobility, involvement with people, recognition, acceptance, freedom from details, contact with people and an open environment that allows them the opportunity to build a social network.

They need public recognition for their accomplishments, which is important for their sense of well-being. They need someone else to do the details. They need a variety of activities, or they will quickly become bored.

I-S BLEND
THE RELATER
Sanguine-Phlegmatic

The I-S (Sanguine-Phlegmatic) is driven by two temperament needs. The primary need is to be accepted socially. The secondary need is to accommodate others. Either need may dominate their behavior depending on the requirements of the situation.

When the "I" and the "S" natural tendencies are combined in the Relater's blend, it produces a people-person who is accommodating to the needs of others.

Relaters are more relationship oriented and consistent compared to the other High "I" blends. The Relater is a frequently found pattern.

DESCRIPTION

The Relater needs to be with people most of the time but some of the time they need to be alone. When alone they will likely rest or sleep. They often become drowsy when sitting still after only a few minutes. They are independent minded and can be very stubborn. Once they establish a routine, it is difficult for them to change. They are very trusting of others and place importance on enduring relationships. It is not unusual for them to keep relationships they formed in kindergarten throughout their lifespan. They are loyal to their friends. They are optimistic and full of hope. Most Relaters smile easily and often.

Relaters have a calming, friendly, accepting expression. They are disarming with their warm, empathic, and understanding approach. Relaters possess a casual kind of poise in social situations. People tend to seek them out, even strangers, to share their problems because they perceive them to be good listeners. Children are easily drawn to them because they feel accepted in their presence. Although doing details and organizational things give them difficulty at times, they can do them quite well. They can be great administrators. Relaters work very well with others because they are optimistic, accepting and accommodating.

STRENGTHS

The Relater naturally and easily forms lasting relationships. They are accepting of others and project a warm, gentle friendliness. They are understanding and compassionate with others.
They are the most consistent of the High "I" blends. Once they establish a routine, they tend to follow it with unyielding determination.

WEAKNESSES

The Relater's effectiveness in relationships and productivity in their career are often hindered because of their reluctance to confront others, their disorganization and impulsiveness. They may play or talk too much. Relaters can be inattentive to details. They may act impulsively without considering the consequences. They can be overly enthusiastic and oversell their ideas.
They can be too optimistic regarding the potential of others. They may overlook obvious flaws in others. The Relater has the natural ability to win friends easily. They naturally project the message that "I want to be your friend." Sometimes they prefer not to be friends, but they do not know how to avoid the relationship without hurting the person's feelings. This can create a dilemma for the Relater.

NEEDS

The Relater will perform at their best and will be highly motivated if their natural, basic needs are met, such as personal involvement with others, the opportunity to form lasting relationships and be recognized for their accomplishments.
They need freedom of expression, to be of service to others, activity and someone else to do the details. They need a routine but with some flexibility and social activity.

I-C BLEND
THE PERFORMER
Sanguine-Melancholy

The I-C (Sanguine-Melancholy) is driven by two temperament needs. The primary need is to be accepted socially. The secondary need is to do things right. Either need may dominate their behavior depending on the requirements of the situation.

When the "I" and the "C" natural tendencies are combined in the Performer's blend, it produces a people-person who is sensitive, creative and detail-oriented. Performers are more formal and sensitive than the other High "I" blends. The Performer is a frequently found pattern.

DESCRIPTION

Performers need to be with people most of the time but some of the time they need to be alone. When alone they will likely think, review, plan, and be creative. They need information, time to think and a plan before they can function effectively. They function best when they have a detailed plan. Once they have a plan, however, they may not be consistent or follow through because of a fear of failure.

Performers have a very active, vivid imagination causing them to be creative in many areas like music, the performing arts, writing, decoration, etc. They tend to be very image conscious and actively seek recognition for their achievements. Performers have a deep need to know that they will be accepted by others. They struggle with guilt feelings. They are usually well organized. Being organized does not necessarily mean that everything is neatly in place. Being organized can also mean that you know where everything is located--if you know what's in the piles, then you're organized!

Information about their job is very important to them, so they may ask many questions before accepting a task. They tend to be cautious because they have a deep need to make a favorable impression. They like status and quality things.

They have difficulty going to sleep because they are thinking too much--reviewing, planning, fretting or creating. The Performer's emotions will likely fluctuate widely, especially if they are embarrassed, or they have been, or may be, rejected. They can do many things to an extreme.

Performers tend to warm up slowly to new people because they are unsure of how they are being received. Once they feel safe or accepted, they become more friendly.

STRENGTHS

The Performer has a natural ability to function well socially (once the fear of rejection has been removed) and privately. They need to be with people, but they also need to spend time alone. Their alone time allows their creativity to be expressed and developed. They process information quickly.

They have the ability to excel in any artistic field. They have a high drive to win. They persuade others with facts and emotion. They are driven to do a task correctly and make a good impression in the process. They are capable of being the best in their chosen field.

WEAKNESSES

The Performer's effectiveness in relationships and productivity in their career is often hindered because of giving into a variety of fears, such as the fear of being rejected, the fear of losing and the fear of being embarrassed or put down.

They often react with extreme emotion if a fear is realized or they perceive something may happen that will be embarrassing. They may demonstrate intense emotion, become critical and condescending and will want to remove themselves from the situation. They also tend to have emotional highs and lows fueled by critical thinking, being impractical, having high standards and failure to spend sufficient time alone.

The Performer, may at times, demonstrate an extreme emotional response and get verbally (sometimes physically) aggressive in response to rejection. This is often followed by remorse and lengthy periods of isolation.

NEEDS

The Performer will be at their best and will be highly motivated if their natural, basic needs are met, such as: being with people, feeling accepted, and spending time alone to think, review, plan and be creative. The amount of daily alone time needed varies with the individual--all need some time alone, but some will need more than others. They need a variety of activities and public recognition for their accomplishments.

HIGH S | PHLEGMATIC

Primary & temperament blends

PATIENT **PASSIVE** POSSESSIVE **TOLERANT** LOYAL **PROCRASTINATES**
SUPPORTIVE **CALM** INDECISIVE **HARMONIOUS** SUBMISSIVE
NEEDS ROUTINE GENTLE **STUBBORN** CORDIAL **AGREEABLE** TEAM-
PLAYER RESISTS CHANGE **PREDICTABLE** ACCOMMODATING

The High "S" (Phlegmatic) is naturally accommodating and service-oriented. They are passive in both favorable and unfavorable environments. They influence their environment by cooperating with others to carry out the task. The High "S" temperament has three combinations and three patterns:

COMBINATION	PATTERN
S-D *(Phlegmatic-Choleric)*	Inspector
S-I *(Phlegmatic-Sanguine)*	Harmonizer
S-C *(Phlegmatic-Melancholy)*	Helper

The traits of the primary temperament, "S," will be altered or modified in some significant way because of the influence of the secondary temperament. Remember, there are at least three levels of intensity of a temperament: classic, moderate, and mild. Some High "S's" will be very strong, others somewhat strong and still others milder.

High "S's" are introverted, calm, unemotional, easygoing, indecisive, patient and agreeable. They are both slow and indirect when responding to others. High "S's" are slow to warm-up but will be accommodating in the process. They are by far the easiest people with whom to get along--as long as you do not try to alter their routine or ask them to change.

High "S's" live a quiet, routine life free of the normal anxieties of the other temperaments. They avoid getting too involved with people, and life in general, preferring a private, low-key life-style centered around home and family.

High "S's" seldom exert themselves with others or push their way along in their career. They just let it happen. They make good team players. They communicate a warm, sincere interest in others, preferring to have just a few close friends. They are possessive of their friendships and material things. High "S's" will be very loyal to their friends and find it difficult to break long-standing relationships regardless of what the other person does or doesn't do. A mother who has the "S" temperament will often refer to her children as, "my children," leaving a bewildered look on her husband's face.

High "S" (Phlegmatic)s will strongly resist sudden change. They need time to adjust when change does occur, especially sudden change. They tend to avoid conflict and will resist making quick decisions. High "S's" are practical, concrete, and traditional thinkers. Their stoic expression often hides their true feelings. They can be grudge holders. High "S's" can also be patient to the point of paralysis. They are persistent and consistent at whatever they undertake. Because of their passive nature, they tend to procrastinate easily and often.

The theologian Ole Hallesby (1962) in *Temperament and the Christian Fatih,* says this about the High "S" (Phlegmatic):

> The phlegmatic has the calm, well-balanced temperament. In the first place, impressions from his surroundings have a far more harmonious effect on the High "S" individual than they have on the other temperaments. There is no one side of his nature that is especially active.

The following represents High "S's" general, but individual differences will occur. What a person is exposed to from an early age plays a vital role in these areas but remember an individual is still responsible for the choices they make. Regardless of one's natural tendencies, discipline applied in any area will control and overcome weaknesses or extreme behavior. The goal is to become a well-balanced person, being in control of thoughts, feelings and behavior.

S-D BLEND
THE INSPECTOR
Phlegmatic-Choleric

The S-D (Phlegmatic-Choleric) blend is driven by two temperament needs. The primary temperament need is to be accommodating. The secondary need is to get results. Either need may dominate their behavior depending on the situation.

When the "S" and the "D" natural tendencies are combined in the Inspector's blend, it produces an accommodating, result-oriented person who is unyielding in their routine and very determined. The Inspector is one of the least frequently found patterns.

DESCRIPTION

Inspectors prefer to be with family or a few close friends most of the time. When focused on a goal they will pursue it with unbending determination. They have an anchored determination to follow their routine or complete a task.

They are accommodating, industrious and independent (loners). The Inspector will have a firm, stoic expression (flat affect) and will rarely smile. They are calm, steady and persevering. They can be very blunt, stubborn and sarcastic. They rarely show emotion or affection.

Inspectors want to operate by themselves and set their pace. Once their mind is made up, they will resist any other method of approach. They seek challenging assignments without close supervision. Inspectors prefer work of a routine and technical nature rather than involvement with people.

This focused individual brings a deceptively intense approach to the task. Being low-key outwardly, their involvement in a task is not easily observed. They are successful because of their commitment to completing a task. After starting a project, they are tenacious and will fight for their objectives. Inspectors are very independent, questioning, and thorough in their approach and will follow through until the task is completed.

Inspectors become sleepy when sitting still after only a few minutes. They are very dependable, routine and loyal (they change their routine slowly). Inspectors are dispassionate anchors of reality. They need time to warm-up before showing friendliness.

STRENGTHS

The Inspector is dependable, determined, and not easily distracted. They are accommodating to a point, as long as it does not interfere with their routine. Once they accept a task, they are unyielding in their commitment to completing it, and they rarely give up. They are loyal to others. They exhibit calmness in a crisis.

WEAKNESSES

The Inspector's effectiveness in relationships and productivity in their career is often hindered because of their resistance to change and bluntness when communicating with others. They project aloofness. They are possessive to a fault and can be very stubborn if it is not their idea. They can be indecisive.

NEEDS

The Inspector will perform at their best and will be highly motivated if their natural, basic needs are met, such as: having a low-key environment, time to change their routine, and clear, specific instructions on when to start and stop a task. They need the opportunity to work steadily toward results. They are very independent and need the freedom to establish their pace.

S-I BLEND
THE HARMONIZER
Phlegmatic-Sanguine

The S-I (Phlegmatic-Sanguine) blend is driven by two temperament needs. The primary temperament need is to be accommodating. The secondary need is to be accepted socially. Either need may dominate their behavior depending on the requirements of the situation.

When the "S" and the "I" natural tendencies are combined in the Harmonizer's blend, it produces an accommodating, people-oriented person who is routine, friendly and tolerant of others. The Harmonizer is the most friendly of the all the High "S" blends. The Harmonizer is a frequently found pattern.

DESCRIPTION

Harmonizers prefer a mostly private, routine existence, and involvement with family and a few friends. The S-I has a stoic expression but will, at times, show a natural smile. They are more friendly than the other High "S" blends. They easily accept others. Harmonizers are accommodating and easy to be associated with both in the work environment and as a friend. They have difficulty confronting or pressuring people. They stubbornly resist change--especially sudden change.

They need some social involvement. Harmonizers are loyal, consistent and dependable. They are naturally service minded. They will often work when they are ill. They are very independent minded and want to operate by themselves and set their pace. They learn by doing (hands-on). They need to be shown how to do a task, and then left alone. Once their mind is made up, they will resist any other method or approach.

Harmonizers can do routine work but will need some change during the day. They have a very difficult time saying no and will often take on more than they can do just to please others. Harmonizers are nice, likable people and have a very pleasant, soft voice. They are more friendly after warming-up and can be very talkative at times.

STRENGTHS

The Harmonizer is naturally accommodating, predictable, and patient. They have a gentle friendliness. They easily accept others, and they are loyal to their family and friends. They are dependable and seek a routine for stability. They avoid conflict, although they can become assertive to restore harmony and peace to their environment.

WEAKNESSES

The Harmonizer's effectiveness in relationships and productivity in their career is often hindered because of their resistance to change, fear of confronting others and indecisiveness. They may try to accommodate or please everyone. They can be very stubborn when asked to change their routine suddenly. They are possessive of relationships and material things. They often lack a sense of urgency to get the task done. They may talk excessively at times.

NEEDS

The Harmonizer will perform at their best and will be highly motivated if their natural, basic needs are met, such as: being of service to others, having a routine schedule, and a specific, concrete plan to follow. They need detailed, specific instructions on when to start and stop a task. They need some social activity and play time.

S-C BLEND
THE HELPER
Phlegmatic-Melancholy

The S-C (Phlegmatic-Melancholy) blend is driven by two temperament needs. The primary temperament need is to be accommodating. The secondary need is to do things right. Either need may dominate their behavior depending on the requirements of the situation.

When the "S" and the "C" natural tendencies are combined in the Helper blend, it produces an accommodating, routine person who is concerned about quality. The Helper is the most consistent of all the High "S" (Phlegmatic) blends. The Helper is a frequently found pattern.

DESCRIPTION

Helpers need to be alone most of the time and spend time with their family at home. They are nice, gracious and cordial people. They rarely show emotion or affection. They are routine, consistent and loyal. They have a strong desire for independence and will resist change, especially sudden change. Helpers are accepting and tolerant of others. They have a stoic expression (flat affect). Helpers are more consistent than the other High "S" blends.

They are naturally routine, accommodating, family-oriented and passive about most things. They are patient, self-controlled and deliberate in their actions. They are amiable and easygoing and slowly pace their way through life. They tend to have a long life-span because they do not get stressed out like the other temperament blends.

This determined and persistent person brings a deceptively intense approach to the task. Being low-key outwardly, their emotional involvement in a task is not easily observed. They are calm, steady and persevering. Helpers are successful because of persistence. After starting a project, they will usually see it through to completion--they rarely give up.

Helpers are independent, questioning and thorough in their approach, and will follow through. They want to operate by themselves and set their pace. Helpers are very possessive of family time, material things and friends. Once their mind is made up, they will resist any other method or approach.

Helpers prefer work of a technical nature and involvement with a limited number of people. Helpers approach a task with calculated moderation. They are always willing to help those they consider to be their friend. They have a difficult time saying no. They have great difficulty confronting or pressuring others, but when they do, they can be sarcastic and slightly offensive. They become sleepy when sitting still after only a few minutes.

STRENGTHS

The Helper is naturally accommodating and service-oriented which promotes their effectiveness in relationships, and productivity in their career. They are calm, patient and loyal. They are accepting of others and possess a gentle, gracious and genuine friendliness. They follow their routine strongly and are therefore predictable and dependable.

WEAKNESSES

The Helper's effectiveness in relationships and productivity in their career are often hindered because of their resistance to change, especially sudden change. They tend to be too accommodating because of their fear of conflict and tension. They recoil at the thought of confronting someone. They tend to worry excessively, and they can be too possessive, stubborn, passive and indecisive.

NEEDS

The Helper will perform at their best and will be highly motivated if their basic, natural needs are met such as: to be of service to others, having a routine, having clear, concrete instructions on when to start and stop a task. They need a low-key environment to have the freedom to be productive (at their pace). They need to be shown how to do a task and then left alone.

HIGH C | MELANCHOLY

Primary & temperament blends

ANALYTICAL **ACCURATE** NEEDS INFORMATION **NEEDS TIME TO THINK** NEEDS A PLAN **NEEDS PRIVACY** CAUTIOUS **CONSIDERATE** COMPETENT **DETAILED** DIPLOMATIC **PICKY** ORGANIZED**INDECISIVE**FACTUAL**CURIOUS**HAS GUILT FEELINGS **CAN BE PESSIMISTIC** CONSCIENTIOUS **LOGICAL**

The High "C" (Melancholy) are detailed-oriented and operate from a plan. They are very private. They influence their environment by adhering to the existing rules and by doing things right. They have a cautious, tentative response designed to reduce tension in an unfavorable environment. After developing a plan, the High "C" can become aggressive to restore peace in an unfavorable situation. The High "C" temperament has three combinations and four common patterns:

COMBINATION	PATTERN
C-D *(Melancholy-Choleric)*	Trainer-Idealist
C-I *(Melancholy-Sanguine)*	Diplomat
C-S *(Melancholy-Phlegmatic)*	Analyst

The traits of the primary temperament, "C," will be altered or modified in some significant way due to the influence of the secondary temperament. Remember, there are at least three levels of intensity of a temperament: classic, moderate, and mild. Some High "C's" will be very strong, others somewhat strong and still others milder.

High "C's" are introverted, logical, analytical, and factual in communication. They need information, time alone to think, and a detailed plan to function effectively without anxiety.

High "C's" respond to others in a slow, cautious, and indirect manner. They are reserved and suspicious until they are sure of your intentions. High "C's" probe for the hidden meaning behind your words. They are timid, may appear unsure, and have a serious expression. High "C's" are self-sacrificing, gifted, and they can be a perfectionist.

High "C's" are conscientious, picky, and can be sensitive to what others think of their work. They have anxiety about the present and future. They tend to have guilt feelings but fail to realize that guilt will not change the past nor will worry change the future. They allow guilt and worry to rob them of enjoying now.

High "C's" are well organized. However, on occasion, they may keep things cluttered, but they will know what is in the piles. They are determined to make the right and best decision so they will collect lots of information and ask very specific questions, and sometimes they will ask the same question several times. They may take excessive time to think through their options before making a decision. Even then, they may not be sure it is the right, and best decision.

High "C's" need reassurance, feedback, and reasons why they should do something. They can be moody, which is usually related to their negative evaluation of people or events.

High "C's" fear taking risks, making wrong decisions, and being viewed as incompetent. They tend to have a negative attitude toward something new until they have had time to think it through. High "C's" are skeptical about almost everything, but they are creative and capable people. They tend to get bored with something once they get it figured out.

The theologian Ole Hallesby (1962) in *Temperament and the Christian Fatih* says this about the High "C" (Melancholy):

> *In this temperament, it is feeling which predominates. Fewer impressions are allowed to enter, but these few are carefully considered and analyzed thoroughly.*

The following represents The High "C" in general, but individual differences will occur. What a person is exposed to from an early age plays a vital role in these areas but remember an individual is still responsible for the choices they make. Regardless of one's natural tendencies, discipline applied in any area will control and overcome weaknesses or extreme behavior. The goal is to become a well-balanced person, being in control of thoughts, feelings and behavior.

C-D BLEND
THE TRAINER
Melancholy-Choleric

The C-D (Melancholy-Choleric) blend is driven by two temperament needs. The primary temperament need is to do things right. The secondary need is to get results. The Trainer, therefore, will influence their environment by striving to do things right while overcoming opposition to get results. Either need may dominate behavior depending on the situation.

When the "C" and the "D" natural tendencies are combined in the Trainer's blend, it produces a detail-oriented person who pushes to get results. Trainers are systematic, precise thinkers, and they follow self-imposed, strict procedures in both their business and personal lives. Trainers have firm, serious expressions, and they rarely smile. The Trainer is a somewhat common pattern.

DESCRIPTION

Trainers are more forceful, pushy and blunt than the other High "C" blends. They have a strong drive to teach others what they know. They can be abrasive and offensive when communicating with others. The Trainer is a systematic, precise thinker who follows procedures in both their business and personal lives. Trainers are attentive to details and push to have things done correctly according to their predetermined standards. They have high standards for themselves and others. They can be a perfectionist about many things. They will resist change until the reasons are explained, defended, and accepted.

They are sensitive and conscientious. They can behave in a diplomatic manner, except when it comes to deviating from standards they have accepted. Trainers can be too forceful in insisting the right way (or their way) be followed.

They are not socially active, preferring work and privacy to being with people. Trainers tend to have difficulty in relationships because they are not flexible and they can be brief and abrasive when communicating with others.

Trainers tend to make decisions slowly because of their need to collect and analyze information (several times) until they are sure of the right and the best course of action.

STRENGTHS

The Trainer is naturally analytical and result-oriented. They are creative problem solvers with high standards. They like to do things right. They have a strong sense of justice (right vs. wrong). They are organized and will operate from a well thought through plan. Once they commit to a goal, they usually follow it to completion.

WEAKNESSES

The Trainer's effectiveness in relationships and productivity in their career is often hindered because of their unrealistic expectations, their high standards and critical attitude. They can be blunt, sarcastic and even condescending when frustrated. They can be abrasive in conversation.

They can be indecisive until they collect sufficient information to make the best decision. The Trainer can be moody which is typically caused by a tendency to think too much about the wrong thing.

NEEDS

The Trainer will perform at their best and will be highly motivated if their natural, basic needs are met, such as: having a structured environment with clear, concrete rules and procedures to follow; having a task that requires working with detail and analysis; having time to collect information, having time alone to think, having time to organize and having time to develop a plan.

The Trainer needs a reason something should be done and will be paralyzed until the task becomes logical to them. They then need feedback and reassurance as they are involved in completing the task to be sure they are proceeding correctly.

C-S-D BLEND
THE IDEALIST
Melancholy-Phlegmatic-Choleric

The C-S-D (Melancholy-Phlegmatic-Choleric) blend is driven by several temperament needs. The primary temperament need is to do things right. The secondary need is to be accommodating. A third temperament need is to get results.

When the High "C" (Melancholy), High "S" (Phlegmatic), and High "D" (Choleric) temperaments are combined in the Idealist's blend, it produces a very detail-oriented person who tries to be accommodating while pushing for results and striving to be perfect in all that they do. These three temperament needs are often in conflict with each other, causing anxiety and stress. This blend is a classic perfectionist.

Idealists are unique because of the influence of the tertiary "D" temperament. It is the influence of this third temperament that causes the Idealist to push their ideal standards to perfection. The Idealist is a somewhat common pattern.

DESCRIPTION

Idealists need information, time alone to think and to develop a plan to guide them in everything they do. They are systematic and precise thinkers. They have high, sometimes unrealistic standards, for themselves and others. They are very attentive to details and push to have things done correctly, according to the standards they have accepted.

Idealists are conscientious in work, requiring accuracy and high standards. They have feelings of guilt and tend to be apologetic about things that are not their fault. They may appear detached or aloof on occasions--this is because they are in deep thought. Idealists normally behave in a diplomatic manner but may become blunt and make condescending remarks if their standards have been violated. Idealists may then become forceful, insisting the right way be followed.

They are not interested in social events, preferring privacy, family, and a few close friends. Idealists make decisions slowly because of their need to collect and analyze information until they are sure of the best and right course of action. They resist change until reasons are explained, defended, and accepted. They have difficulty going to sleep because they are analyzing what happened yesterday, or today, or what will happen tomorrow or next week. They are also planning their activities for the next day.

STRENGTHS

The Idealist is a natural perfectionist. They are logical, analytical, tenacious and strive to do everything exactly right. They push to maintain very high standards in everything they do. They like to follow predetermined procedures so they will not make a mistake. They are organized and usually neat. They have a strong sense of justice and will fight for a cause.

WEAKNESSES

The Idealist's effectiveness in relationships and productivity in their career is often hindered because of their high standards and unrealistic expectations. They are inflexible and resist change until they've had time to think about it several times. They tend to be critical of others, moody, and indecisive.

They are easily frustrated and exhibit a demeaning attitude and may withdraw when things do not go their way. They rehearse negative self-talk that keeps them from enjoying the moment--they worry about what should have been and what could have been. They seem never satisfied with who they are or where they are in life. They continue to seek perfection but never seem to achieve the ideal they so strongly desire. It's like a donkey walking toward the carrot that is dangling at the end of a stick. The stick is tied to their back and hanging over their head--the donkey moves and the carrot moves. Perfection will be achieved only when the donkey gets the carrot! Since you cannot live perfectly in an imperfect world, do your best, and that will always be enough.

NEEDS

The Idealist will perform at their best and will be highly motivated if their natural, basic needs are met, such as: being able to collect information, having time alone to analyze and plan, having concrete, clear rules and procedures and having a detailed plan to follow. The Idealist needs a structured environment and procedures to follow, or they cannot function effectively. Without these needs being met, the Idealist will experience a high degree of anxiety.

C-I BLEND
THE DIPLOMAT
Melancholy-Sanguine

The C-I (Melancholy-Sanguine) blend is driven by two temperament needs. The primary temperament need is to do things right. The secondary need is to be accepted socially. Either need may dominate their behavior depending on the requirements of the situation.

When the "C" and the "I" natural tendencies are combined in the Diplomat's blend, it produces a detail-oriented person who enjoys some social activity. The Diplomat is the most friendly of all the High "C" blends. The Diplomat is a frequently found pattern.

DESCRIPTION

Diplomats need to be alone most of the time, and they need to be with people some of the time. When alone they will likely review the day and plan tomorrow. Diplomats are more friendly than the other High "C" blends, and they have a natural smile. They are analytical, systematic and sensitive to the needs of others. This is a versatile, productive individual who works well with most everyone. Diplomats like to have fun and laugh when they feel comfortable and accepted. They can be very talkative at times. They have high personal ambitions but often fail to achieve their dreams because of their fear of failure.

Diplomats tend to be well-balanced, and they are precise thinkers who tend to follow procedures in both their business and personal lives. They are mostly well organized and are attentive to detail. Diplomats can be openly friendly at times. They will be more friendly toward new people after they warm up. They like to do things correctly according to their standards. They like quality and status things. They are very conscientious. Diplomats need some mobility rather than sitting for long periods of time. They can be very sensitive to criticism and react with strong emotion.

Diplomats make decisions slowly because they are analyzing their options. They need to be sure of the right, and best course of action, especially when involved in a new project.

At times, they may have difficulty going to sleep due to excessive worry. They like to ease into the day instead of rushing into activity. They prefer others to wait awhile before talking to them after they awaken. The Diplomat struggles with having guilt feelings, even about something that is not their fault. They tend to be apologetic.

STRENGTHS

The Diplomat is naturally private, analytical, while they enjoy being socially active some of the time. Most of their social activity will be with family and friends rather than with new people and groups. They are gentle and diplomatic when dealing with people. They are conscientious, thoughtful, and good at solving people problems. They have a desire for quality in whatever they do and they are creative. They can make an impressively detailed presentation to a group. They make excellent teachers.

WEAKNESSES

The Diplomat's effectiveness in relationships and productivity in their career is often hindered because of their indecisiveness, sensitivity, unrealistic expectations and high standards. They can be moody and inflexible. They can also be critical of others and, at times, they talk too much. They tend to withdraw under pressure and will avoid confronting others.

NEEDS

Diplomats are motivated to perform at their best if their natural, basic needs are met, such as: a structured environment with clear procedures to follow, some social contact with people and some flexibility in their schedule. They become restless if they have to sit for long periods of time to do a task. They need time alone to think, analyze and to develop a plan.

C-S BLEND
THE ANALYST
Melancholy-Phlegmatic

The C-S (Melancholy-Phlegmatic) blend is driven by two temperament needs. The primary temperament need is to do things right. The secondary need is to be accommodating. Either need may dominate their behavior depending on the requirements of the situation. When the "C" and the "S" natural tendencies are combined in the Analyst's blend, it produces a detail-oriented person who is accommodating and will cautiously plan their way through life. The Analyst is the most consistent of all the High "C" (Melancholy) blends. The Analyst is a frequently found pattern.

DESCRIPTION

Analysts prefer being alone most of the time. They are not socially active, preferring to be with family or a few close friends. When at a social event they usually do not stay for a long time. To function well, they need information, time alone to think and a plan from which to operate. They like working privately on a project. They are usually very well organized and tend to operate from a list--it may be written down or just in their head. If they are not neatly organized, they know what's in those piles!

Analysts are pleasant and accommodating people who tend to seek a structured environment requiring attention to detail. They have a self-sacrificing, self-critical nature and struggle with guilt feelings about things that are not their fault. Analysts are more conscientious and private than the other High "C" blends. They are systematic, precise thinkers who tend to follow procedures in both their business and personal lives. They will withdraw from aggressive people. They will have difficulty putting pressure on others. The Analyst will become aggressive to restore harmony to their environment.

Analysts make decisions slowly because of their need to collect and review information until they are sure of the right and best course of action. This is especially true when involved in a new project. They will be a bit of a perfectionist at times but not like the Idealist pattern.

Analysts are good at anticipating problems and figuring out solutions, but not good at taking action. Analysts have difficulty going to sleep because they are thinking.

Analysts feel safe to think, review and plan when they stay up after the rest of the family has gone to bed. Males in particular like staying up late at night to flip through the TV channels. Someone said that men do not want to watch TV, they just want to see what's on the next channel!

They have a strong sense of justice. They like quality things. They resist change until reasons are explained, defended and accepted. They resist changing their plan, especially if the change is sudden. They need pushing to be sociable beyond their family and close friends. The Analyst often has a High "I" as a close friend because they like their fun nature and carefree attitude.

STRENGTHS

The Analyst has a natural drive to analyze everything and operate from a detailed plan and list. They like to do things right according to predetermined rules and procedures. They are well organized and give attention to detail. They are usually diplomatic when dealing with others. They are quietly creative and good at solving technical problems. They work well alone. If they have respect for those with whom they are associated, they will cooperate and be a good, helpful team member.

WEAKNESSES

The Analyst's effectiveness in relationships and productivity in their career is often hindered because of their negative self-talk, critical attitude and being too sensitive. They often fail to take action on their detailed plan because they are never sure if they have all the necessary information. They often have unrealistic expectations for themselves and others. They can be moody and will withdraw to be alone to think. They often bring misery upon themselves because of being too picky and having a negative view of people, events and life in general.

NEEDS

The Analyst will perform at their best and will be highly motivated if their natural, basic needs are met, such as: having a structured environment with clear rules and procedures to follow, having time to organize, having time to gather information and having time to think and develop a plan. They need detailed work and privacy. They need feedback and reassurance that what they are doing is appropriate and acceptable. Once they accept the feedback and reassurance they have received, they will continue and move forward with efficiency.

Chapter Six

STEP TWO: SELF ACCEPTANCE

Accept your temperament blend

The second step in becoming a ***better you*** is to *accept* your natural temperament tendencies. As you become aware of your temperament blend, it is normal to like and embrace some of your tendencies and dislike and resist accepting other aspects with which you were born. Acceptance does not mean that you must resign yourself to always live with the limitations that exist with your temperament. Every temperament blend has limitations and weaknesses which can be controlled and their impact reduced or eliminated. This will be discussed in the next chapter.

FOUR REASONS TO ACCEPT YOUR TEMPERAMENT BLEND

1. YOU WERE BORN WITH YOUR TEMPERAMENT BLEND

There are two basic theories as to the origin of one's personality. It is either there at birth or acquired by chance.

Born as a blank slate. Aristotle held the position that the mind at birth is a blank slate (from the Latin, *tabula rasa*) on which experience would determine an individual's personality. This position essentially teaches that everyone is born without a personality or built-in mental content. An individual's personality or identity is determined completely by chance, based on experiences after birth. It is formed as the individual responds and interacts with the variables in their unique situation.

Temperament is Inborn. This position teaches that a person is born with a basic temperament and that the traits are developed according to that person's response to their environment. Jules Asher concludes in his article "Born to be Shy?":

> "*Today, however, evidence from several lines of research indicates that at least some behavioral traits such as extreme shyness are enduring aspects*

*of personality that are grounded in inborn ways of responding physiologically
to the environment. In short, they're part of some people's basic temperament."*

Dr. Tim LaHaye in *Understanding The Male Temperament* states,

*"The combination of inherited traits he receives from his parents at the
time of conception will determine his eventual temperament."*

In her research featured in Dr. Robert White's book, *Abnormal Personality*,
Margaret Fries discovered that infants within the first ten days of life could be
classified as quiet, moderately active or active. These differences were stable and
could be observed five years later. This research shows that behavioral tendencies
are present from birth.

Finally, ask any mother that has raised at least two children and chances are
she will tell you they were different from the beginning. A mother of two told
me one of her children was active, friendly and smiled a lot just after birth. Whereas
the other child was shy and frightened when strangers were present. This suggests
that we are all born with certain traits of behavior that are observable in the early
days of life.

The conclusion is that it is common sense and undeniable that people are
born with different tendencies referred to in this work as *temperament*. I believe
each person receives their temperament blend by Divine appointment. This was
recognized thousands of years ago and recorded in Psalms 139:14-16; *"I praise you
because I am fearfully and wonderfully made; your works are wonderful, I know that
full well. My frame was not hidden from you when I was made in the secret place
when I was woven together in the depths of the earth. Your eyes saw my unformed
body; all the days ordained for me were written in your book before one of them came
to be."*

2. IT LEADS TO SELF-ACCEPTANCE

The second reason to accept the temperament blend you were born with is that
it leads to self-acceptance. Maxwell Maltz states:

*"You as a personality are not in competition with any other personality
simply because there is not another person on the face of the earth like you,
or in your particular class. You are an individual. You are unique. You
are not 'like' any other person and cannot become 'like' any other person.
You are not 'supposed' to be like any other person, and no other person is*

'supposed' to be like you."

There are many areas of *self* that need to be accepted to have a healthy self-concept, such as heritage, physical appearance, and innate abilities. Some of these can be changed to some degree while others cannot. A healthy self-concept will depend mostly on your acceptance of what you cannot change and a decision to change the things you can. One area of self that is necessary to understand and accept is *temperament*. It is the foundation upon which all else is built. You were born with your temperament, and it is the one that you are *supposed* to have.

3. YOU HAVE A TEMPERAMENT COMFORT ZONE

A third reason for accepting your temperament is you have a comfort zone of behavior that fits you best.

There is a way of behaving that you feel is right, good and normal. This comfort zone represents your temperament, and it is the way you naturally think, feel and behave. For example, the High "I" (Sanguine) prefers social activity and the High "C" (Melancholy) prefers being alone. Both represent normal desires or comfort zones of behavior, *and* both are acceptable and okay. Dr. John Geier states:

> *"During a lifetime we experience many emotions, but there is an emotional state which is most characteristic for each of us. We depart from that basic temperament when aroused by such feelings as love, hate, sadness, anger, rage, or exuberance. However, these emotions tend to be as transient as they are intense. Love slips through our fingers; hate is difficult to sustain for long periods; joy and sorrow eventually dissipate. Like strong winds, these emotions temporarily ruffle the surface of our usual emotional demeanor. When others describe us with such words as friendly, logical, aggressive, or careful, they are referring to the feeling state we usually project. That state reflects our self-concept and has evolved from genetic predispositions and the shaping forces of the environment. Others may approve or disapprove of our temperament. It may meld or conflict with the expectations of groups or organizations. The crucial aspect is recognizing the 'given' of our emotions and choosing the environment in which we will be accepted and productive."*

Whatever your temperament, it is perfectly normal to reflect it in your daily behavior.

Temperament is determined in the same manner as hair color, eye color, bone structure, etc. You were born with it and it will never change. A High "D" (Choleric) will never become a High "C" (Melancholy) or any other temperament. That is not possible, just as it is impossible to change your basic body structure with which you were born.

Therefore, you are normal. You have natural strengths and weaknesses, so it is okay to be you. You do not have to pretend to be someone else. I am not suggesting that you always demonstrate the traits of your temperament or that it is permissible to overlook areas that you need to control. I *am* saying that you need to behave like a controlled, mature person regardless of your temperament. Here are some reasons why you should relax and be yourself:

You are the most *comfortable* when you are behaving in a manner that represents the controlled strengths of your temperament.

You are *perceived in the best possible manner* when you are expressing the controlled strengths of your temperament.

You have your most *positive impact* upon others when you are expressing the controlled strengths of your temperament.

You are the most *effective* and *efficient* in life when you are expressing the controlled strengths of your temperament.

You are at your *best* when you are expressing the controlled strengths of your temperament. Relax and enjoy being who you were designed to be.

4. THERE IS NOT A BEST TEMPERAMENT

No matter what your temperament blend is, you can achieve as much success as you desire and your talents will allow:

*It does not matter what you are; what matters
is what you do with what you are!*

The High "D" (Choleric) will become successful by taking risks. The High "I" (Sanguine) will be successful working with people. The High "S" (Phlegmatic) will be successful being consistent and not giving up. The High "C" (Melancholy) will be successful having a detailed plan.

SUMMARY

You are normal. Your temperament was predetermined, just as were your hair color, eye color, and bone structure. You were born with your temperament, and it will remain with you throughout your lifespan. Since you have normal, natural strengths and weaknesses, accept the temperament with which you were born and enjoy being who you were designed to be.

Chapter Seven

STEP THREE: SELF EXPRESSION

Express your temperament blend

The third step to becoming a ***better you***, is to express your natural temperament tendencies. Each temperament has natural strengths that are unique to that temperament. This means you do some things naturally well *and* better than the other three temperaments. For example, the High "D" (Choleric) naturally influences others by getting results quickly and moving to the next task. The High "I" (Sanguine) naturally influences others by getting people together to socialize. The High "S" (Phlegmatic) naturally influences others by having a routine and having a desire to accommodate others. The High "C" (Melancholy) naturally influences others by doing details and having a plan. Once you understand your natural tendencies with which you were born, relax and enjoy being who you were designed to be.

STAY WITHIN YOUR NATURAL STRENGTHS

You are the most comfortable *and* effective when you are operating within the controlled strengths of your temperament blend. When you are fearful, angry or trying to be deceptive, you step outside of your natural strengths and become uncomfortable and less effective. When you express negative emotions, you will be perceived as unnatural and disingenuous, and therefore, your communication will not be well received.

I am not saying that it is always inappropriate to express negative emotions and behavior that is deceptive. There are times when it is appropriate and even necessary to be fearful, angry and deceptive. For example, when you are faced with imminent physical harm, all three may be necessary to survive or escape.

I am saying that in our normal interaction with others, negative emotions and attempts to deceive will project a message that is unnatural and, therefore, ineffective.

BECOME AWARE

The message that everyone projects is a combination of words, attitudes, tone of voice and body language. Be aware that an effective message occurs when you are behaving in a manner that represents the *controlled strengths* of your temperament. Your message will be perceived as natural, and others will see you as being genuine, authentic, relaxed, not pretending and trustworthy. You will be perceived as being comfortable with who you are and others will hear what you have to say.

When a **High "D"** (*Choleric*) is operating within the controlled strengths of their temperament, they normally have a confident and firm look on their face. Their body language is strong, erect and unyielding. They use powerful words and say them with command and authority in their voice. They have a fast and assertive pace. The High "D" has a positive impact on others when they are being decisive, seeking results and solving a problem.

When a **High "I"** (*Sanguine*) is operating within the controlled strengths of their temperament, they normally have a receptive, inviting and warm look on their face. Their body language is open, and their gestures are friendly and inviting. They use exciting words, talk a lot, smile and have a fast and friendly pace. The High "I" is winsome and they have a positive impact on others when they are enthusiastic and sociable.

When a **High "S"** (*Phlegmatic*) is operating within the controlled strengths of their temperament, they normally have a stoic expression on their face. Their body language is non-threatening, easygoing, soft and they are not animated. The High "S" has a positive impact on others when they are accommodating and consistent.

When a **High "C"** (*Melancholy*) is operating within the controlled strengths of their temperament, they normally have a serious expression on their face. Their body language is guarded, and they use very precise words. The High "C" has a positive impact on others when they are doing things right, being organized, being thoughtful and being creative.

USE YOUR STRENGTHS

Based on the temperament blend you identified as your own in Chapter 4, answer the following questions:

What are three strengths that you appreciate the most about yourself?

1._____
2._____
3. _____

How can each of these strengths help you become more effective in life?

1. _____
2. _____
3. _____

What is the one strength that you feel has the greatest impact on others?

_____

How can you use this strength to have a more effective impact on others?

_____

SUMMARY

Everyone projects a message that represents their natural temperament tendencies.

Communication with others is *ineffective* when your tone of voice and body language project anger, fear or deception. Communication with others is *effective* when you are relaxed, not angry or fearful, and you are gracious, matter-of-fact and your body language is open.

When you express your temperament tendencies in a controlled manner, your communication will be received with confidence, and you will promote positive behavior in others.

Relax, be natural, be yourself and consciously operate out of the controlled strengths of your temperament blend. Say what you think absent of negative emotions and you will have a positive impact on others.

Chapter Eight

STEP FOUR: SELF-CONTROL

Overcome your natural weaknesses

The fourth step to becoming a **better you** is to choose to control and overcome your natural temperament weaknesses. Ole Hallesby said, *"To be sure, we can, with mind and will, affect our temperament; and indeed, we should do so"* (Hallesby, p. 10). These words sum up the task we all face--to control and overcome a given weakness by engaging our mind and our will.

In the last chapter, you were encouraged to be yourself and express the controlled strengths of your temperament. In this chapter, you are being encouraged to overcome your natural weaknesses.

Never condemn yourself because you have a certain weakness or several for that matter. Being human means it is normal to have weaknesses. It is not inappropriate to have these weaknesses, but it is *immature* not to work at controlling and overcoming them. Dr. Henry Brandt said, in his unpublished notes, *"A mature man is one who is sufficiently objective about himself to know both his strengths and weaknesses and to create a planned program for overcoming his weaknesses."* As discussed in the previous chapter, when you are operating out of natural strengths, you project an *effective* message to others. Conversely, if you are operating out of your natural weaknesses, the message you project to others is *ineffective*.

AN INEFFECTIVE MESSAGE

An *ineffective* message occurs when you operate outside of your natural tendencies and behave in a manner that represents the weaknesses of your temperament blend.

When behaving outside the controlled strengths of your temperament blend, others will perceive you as trying to be someone or something that you are not. A natural, *effective* message will also become distorted when one expresses strong emotions, such as anger and fear. Such a person has a negative impact on others. Dr. William M. Marston said in *Emotions of Normal People*;

"I do not regard you as a normal person, emotionally, when you are suffering from fear, rage, pain, shock, desire to deceive, or any other emotional state whatsoever containing turmoil and conflict. Your emotional responses are normal when they produce pleasantness and harmony" (Marston, p.12).

When you display inappropriate emotions, it shows in your attitude, tone of voice and body language. It is then filtered through your temperament blend and produces an *offensive* message.

When you express anger, others will likely become defensive, be offended and withdraw. When you express fear, others will likely sense a lack of confidence in what you are saying. When you are deceptive, others will likely be suspicious of your intentions.

The following is what happens when the various temperaments fail to exercise self-control and express anger, fear or try to deceive.

THE HIGH "D" (CHOLERIC)

When a High "D" expresses the weaknesses of their temperament, they intimidate and frighten others. Their body language projects anger, rejection and no concern for others. Their message is that they are in control, unyielding and will win regardless of the cost. They speak with powerful, negative words, and their voice reflects forceful command and authority.

When a High "D" cannot get results fast enough, lose control, or have been taken advantage of, they may do the following:

Have a sudden burst of anger	Be abrupt and blunt
Become annoyed	Show a lack of sensitivity and empathy
Become abrasive and critical	Be impatient with others
Be dictatorial	Procrastinate

When these behaviors occur, the High "D"'s *effectiveness* is greatly diminished. Such behavior has a negative impact on others and ignites the fight or flight response. People will either stand their ground and give back the same emotion they are getting, *or* they will shut down out of fear that more of the same will continue if they respond.

The High "D" needs to realize that demonstrating such behavior may appear to get them what they want at the moment, but it destroys communication and damages relationships.

THE HIGH "I" (SANGUINE)

When a High "I" is expressing the weaknesses of their temperament, they project emotional disapproval of others. When angry, their body language is closed, and their gestures are negative. They often withdraw to show their feelings of disapproval. When trying to deceive others, they are capable of being charming and complimentary to get what they want. When fearful, they are capable of having a strong emotional outburst.

When a High "I" is embarrassed, rejected, disrespected or viewed as not being important, they may do the following:

Be angry and/or critical	Subtly rebel
Verbally attack	Procrastinate
Deny facts and reality	Talk excessively
Manipulate with emotion	Have a sudden shift in mood
Become depressed and withdraw	

When these behaviors occur, the High "D's" effectiveness is greatly diminished. Such behavior has a negative impact on others and ignites the *fight or flight* response. People will either stand their ground and give back the same emotion they are getting, or they will shut down out of fear that more of the same will continue if they respond.

The High "I" needs to realize that demonstrating such behavior may appear to get them what they want at the moment, but it destroys relationships and damages self-esteem.

THE HIGH "S" (PHLEGMATIC)

When a High "S" is expressing the weaknesses of their temperament, they project disapproval of others by becoming sarcastic and passively aggressive. Their body language is closed, and their gestures are negative. To show their disapproval, they will slow down, become quiet, withdraw, be late for an appointment or stubbornly resist fulfilling a request. They will comply outwardly but rebel inwardly. Their actions will be subtle but defiant without emotion. When a High "S" experiences conflict, sudden change, confrontation, disharmony or they have to put pressure on people, they may do the following:

Passively resist	Become paralyzed
Become indecisive	Withdraw and worry
Become too accommodating	Sleep more
Procrastinate	Become sarcastic

When these behaviors occur, the High "S's" *effectiveness* is greatly diminished. Such behavior has a negative impact on others and causes frustration and confusion. People will push more to get a response, causing more resistance (push back).

The High "S" needs to realize that demonstrating such behavior does not resolve the issue and causes frustration in others.

THE HIGH "C" (MELANCHOLY)

When a High "C" is expressing the weaknesses of their temperament, they project disapproval of others by being critical and demeaning. Their body language is closed, and their gestures are negative. Their body language will project fear and concern. They will likely demonstrate strong, negative emotions and then withdraw to fume. The High "C" has a negative impact on others by insisting that their way is followed without compromise.

When a High "C" experiences being wrong, having their work criticized, losing control, having conflict, being pushed to complete a project, not having enough information or they have to put pressure on people, they may do the following:

Withdraw	Become negative and suspicious
Have a critical attitude	Become verbally aggressive
Show excessive sensitivity	Become depressed and want to quit
Procrastinate	Analyze more to be sure they are right

When these behaviors occur, the High "C's" effectiveness is greatly diminished. Such behavior has a negative impact and causes others to be frustrated because their opinion is not valued. Others will consider the High "C" to be rigid and unreasonable.

The High "C" needs to realize that demonstrating such behavior is viewed as selfish, controlling and divisive.

WHAT YOU MAY GET

When you express the weaknesses of your temperament blend, your message will *not* be well received and you will likely ignite negative behavior in others. Here's how the recipients of your negative behavior will likely respond:

> *The High "D" (Choleric)* | may get aggressive especially if you take issue with them personally.

> *The High "I" (Sanguine)* | will feel rejected or embarrassed and they may get very emotional and verbally abusive.

> *The High "S" (Phlegmatic)* | will be frightened, withdraw and be accommodating to avoid conflict and confrontation.

> *The High "C" (Melancholy)* | will feel misunderstood, get defensive, get depressed and then want to quit.

Decide to overcome the weaknesses of your temperament blend so that you will have a positive impact on others and the intent of your communication will be received.

OVERCOME YOUR WEAKNESSES

It was said three thousand years ago that people find what they are looking for: Proverbs 11:27 states, *"He who earnestly seeks good finds favor, but trouble will come to him who seeks evil."* This proverb contrasts one who seeks good to the one who seeks evil. **Notice that both will *find* what they are looking for.**

If you want to overcome your weaknesses, you must be willing to seek different behavior. It may sound simple; however this is the most difficult step to take. You have to *decide* and *define* the kind of person you want to be. That decision will determine the goals that you set for yourself. Since all behavior is goal directed, then all behavior is a choice. So make a choice to overcome your weaknesses and to use goal setting and affirmations to become a *better* you!

MOTIVATION

To be fully motivated to change, you must use your will, mind and emotions.

> *Will* | You must first decide that you *want* to overcome a specific weakness.

That sounds elementary, but it the most difficult step to take. Suppose you have identified a specific weakness that you want to overcome. You may be thinking, "I would like to overcome the grip this weakness has on me, so I'm going to *try* really hard." If this is your approach, then you will surely fail because these words do not reflect a decision to overcome the weakness. You cannot say, "I would *like* to do this so I will *try* hard." To say that you are going to *try* really hard, is to give yourself an out if you do not overcome the weakness. Your rational would then be, "Well, *I did try!*" When a decision is made to overcome the weakness, your self-talk will be, "I will overcome my weakness."

> *Mind* | Once you have made the decision to change, you must now engage your thoughts on how to accomplish your goal which is achieved through self-talk and visualization.

You must now use positive self-talk and build pictures in your mind, seeing yourself successfully overcoming your weakness.

> *Emotions* | Now get excited! You will know that you are fully involved when you are excited about overcoming your weakness.

GOAL SETTING

Establish a goal to overcome a specific weakness that you have identified is interfering with your personal growth and effectiveness. Write down your goal in one sentence and review it daily. The value of goal setting cannot be underestimated as Paul J. Meyer states in Dynamics of Goal Setting:

> *"Goal setting is undoubtedly the most important single ingredient in both self-motivation and successful achievement. It always has been and always will be! Goal setting alone has the capacity to span the chasm between a wish and its fulfillment."*

AFFIRMATIONS

The use of affirmations is based on the understanding that everyone talks to themselves, continuously. Positive affirmations help you say the right things when you talk to yourself. The daily use of affirmations will remind you of the kind of person you want to become. Proverbs 23:7 says, *"For as he thinketh in his heart, so is he."* If you repeat the positive affirmation that represents the change you desire, you will eventually become what the affirmation represents.

Put your affirmations on 3x5 cards and keep them with you to review at least three times a day (morning, noon and in the evening just before you go to sleep). Someone has said, "We need to be told once, but reminded often," so repeat your affirmations for at least 30 days or until the new tendency becomes automatic in your behavior.

FACE YOUR WEAKNESSES

Embracing your weaknesses is like someone using a cattle prod on you; it's painful at first, but useful to move you along on your journey. The weaknesses listed on the following pages are common to the four temperaments. More can be said about each weakness, so take ownership and pursue an in-depth study in a particular area of concern. You may also wish to discuss your weaknesses with one whom you trust and who would be objective with you, but not condescending.

Select from the weaknesses noted on the following pages the ones that you need to overcome. Be objective and honest with yourself and remember never to condemn yourself for having a weakness. Use affirmations until you have modified your behavior. The reward for such effort will be a more efficient, effective, balanced life and you will have a positive impact on others.

COMMON TEMPERAMENT WEAKNESSES

CONTROLLING

To be *controlling* can be defined as *exercising restraint or dominance over someone; to make decisions for another person.*

> *The High "D" (Choleric)* | may control people and events because they think that their way is the only way; they do not want to be taken advantage of; they do not value or care what others think.

> *The High "I" (Sanguine)* | may control people and events because they are protecting their image or they are trying to make a favorable impression.

> *The High "S" (Phlegmatic)* | may control people and events because they are trying to prevent change or avoid conflict.

The High "C" (Melancholy) | may control people and events because they believe that their way is the best since they have thought about it deeply.

If this is your weakness, realize that this kind of control over others reveals arrogance, hostility and a lack of respect for individuality. Controlling people believe that they are superior to the one being controlled. Being controlled causes others to be frustrated, feel resentment and feel devalued as a person. It prevents others from expressing their creativity and individuality. Being a controlling person alienates others and causes them to withdraw and withhold information. It produces dependence, prevents independent thinking and harms relationships.

To overcome this weakness, first accept ownership of your *choice* to be controlling. Second, establish a *goal* to overcome this weakness. Third, *use affirmations daily* to be reminded of what needs to be done to overcome this weakness. Here are some suggestions:

"I encourage independent thinking."
"I value other people's opinions."
"I do not control people and events."
"I allow people to make their own mistakes."
"I allow people to creatively accomplish the task."

IMPATIENT

To be *impatient* can be defined *as an irritation or lack of tolerance with anyone or anything that causes delay.*

The High "D" (Choleric) | may become impatient when; people do not respond quickly to their requests or demands; results are not coming quickly enough; they have unrealistic standards being imposed on others; they value quick results more than they value and respect people.

The High "I" (Sanguine) | may become impatient when; a situation begins to unfold that will cause them embarrassment; they cannot get instant gratification; others will not conform to their wishes.

The High "S" (Phlegmatic) | may become impatient when; a routine is about to change, their peaceful home life has been interrupted, or conflict occurs.

The High "C" (Melancholy) | may become impatient when; their plan is interrupted, or they are pushed to complete a project while they are still collecting and analyzing information. They also show impatience when attending a social event, especially being around people they do not know.

If this is your weakness, realize that being impatient with people shows a lack of respect and causes frustration and resentment. Being impatient alienates people, harms relationships and shows an unwillingness to delay gratification. Impatient people instantly resent being denied their desire, regardless of the reason. Being impatient means that instant gratification is more important than self-control. Impatience is a form of anger.

To overcome this weakness, first accept ownership of your *choice* to be impatient. Second, establish a *goal* to overcome this weakness. Third, use *affirmations daily* to be reminded of what needs to be done to overcome this weakness. Here are some suggestions:

"I am patient with others."
"I value and respect people."
"I delay gratification."
"I allow people time to accomplish a task."
"I control my emotions when things do not happen quickly."

The virtue of having patience has been woven throughout literature for thousands of years. Consider Proverbs 19:11 which states, *"A man's wisdom gives him patience; it is to his glory to overlook an offense."*

EXPLOSIVE

To be explosive can be defined as *suddenly expressing inappropriate, strong emotions.*

The High "D" (Choleric) | is naturally quickly aroused but easily calmed. They may, however, explode suddenly when; they are not getting the immediate results they want; someone is not submitting to them; they perceive that they are being taken advantage of; they have been verbally attacked.

The High "I" (Sanguine) | may explode suddenly when they have been embarrassed or rejected; they perceive they have been disrespected; or they have failed at accomplishing something.

The High "S" (Phlegmatic) | will rarely explode emotionally, but when they do, it is usually related to experiencing sudden change or something has happened to their family.

The High "C" (Melancholy) | may explode suddenly if someone tries to change their plans without giving a reason or their work has been criticized.

If this is your weakness, realize that suddenly exploding causes people to withdraw, be fearful, and feel devalued. It reveals arrogance, hostility and a lack of respect for others. Explosive people refuse to control their impulses.

To overcome this weakness, first accept ownership of your *choice* to be explosive. Second, establish a *goal* to overcome this weakness. Third, *use affirmations daily* to be reminded of what needs to be done to overcome this weakness. Here are some suggestions:

> *"I control my emotions."*
> *"I am patient with people."*
> *"I do not consistently control people and events."*
> *"I allow people to make their own mistakes."*

> *"Be completely humble and gentle; be patient, bearing with one another in love."* (Ephesians 4:2 NIV)

> *"Do not let any unwholesome talk come out of your mouths, but only what is helpful for building others up according to their needs, that it may benefit those who listen."* (Ephesians 4:29 NIV)

> *"Do not be deceived: God cannot be mocked. A man reaps what he sows. Whoever sows to please their flesh, from the flesh will reap destruction; whoever sows to please the Spirit, from the Spirit will reap eternal life. Let us not become weary in doing good, for at the proper time we will reap a harvest if we do not give up."* (Galatians 6:7-9 NIV)

FEAR OF REJECTION

The fear of being *rejected* is defined as an *excessive amount of anxious concern that one may be shunned or disrespected by another; one may not be well received by another; one may be looked upon unfavorably if they are the cause of a loss.* Most everyone has some fear of being rejected, but it is a lifestyle problem when it occurs frequently.

The High "D" (Choleric) | will rarely experience a fear of being rejected. If it does happen, they are capable of laying the incident aside quickly and moving on to whatever is next in their journey through life. They are so forward thinking that they quickly forget a disappointment.

The High "I" (Sanguine) | when the High "I" perceives that they have been or may be rejected, there may be a sudden eruption of emotion with verbal rebuke. In extreme reactions, the High "I" may become physically aggressive.

The High "S" (Phlegmatic) | will likely withdraw, become depressed, and will sleep more than usual. They will have difficulty expressing their feelings, even to those they trust. They tend to hang on to negative feelings for a long time.

The High "C" (Melancholy) | will likely withdraw, become, angry, get depressed, and sleep *less* than usual. The High "C" will relive the event over and over and think of things that can be done to reverse the situation. It is very difficult for the High "C" to deal with rejection, they will likely pout for a long time.

If this is your weakness, realize that your fear of rejection is holding you back from becoming a *better you*. The direction of your life is being guided by what you fear. To have this kind of excessive fear is to place an inordinate amount of importance upon *self*. A person that has an excessive fear of rejection has an inflated and unhealthy concern over what other people think of them. When a person places too much importance on their image, they have an unrealistic expectation that they are to be treated with respect by everyone and in every situation. Such a person is self-centered.

To overcome this weakness, first accept ownership of your *choice* to fear rejection. Second, establish a *goal* to overcome your fear. Third, use affirmations daily to be reminded of what needs to be done to overcome your fear. Here are some suggestions:

> *"I do not take rejection personally."*
> *"I accept rejection as an opportunity to learn and grow."*
> *"I will respond with acceptance."*
> *"I control my emotions."*

> *"Do not be anxious about anything, but in every situation, by prayer and petition, with thanksgiving, present your requests to God. And the peace of God, which transcends all understanding, will guard your hearts and your minds in Christ Jesus."* (Philippians 4:6-7 NIV)

INDECISIVE

To be *indecisive* is defined as *the lack of willingness to come to a conclusion or to make a choice.*

The High "D" (Choleric) | is by far the most decisive of the four temperaments; they can make decisions quickly for others as well. Once they make a decision they do not review or revisit their choice. They rarely regret a decision they've made because they are forward thinking.

The High "I" (Sanguine) | when the High "I" hesitates to make a decision, they are usually concerned about how the decision will make them look in the eyes of others. They weigh their choices carefully to reduce the possibility of failing.

The High "S" (Phlegmatic) | is the most indecisive of the four temperaments. Before they make a decision, they need to know that everyone will be pleased. If a conflict is possible, they will put off making the decision. They also make decisions that will be best for their family.

The High "C" (Melancholy) | will be indecisive until they have collected enough information and have taken the time to analyze what it means. Even then they may not be sure until they've analyzed what they just analyzed.

To make a decision sometimes requires taking the time to analyze the facts so that you can make the best possible choice. To be *routinely* indecisive about most anything will interfere with you becoming a *better you.*

If this is your weakness, realize that it not only hurts you, but it causes others to be frustrated waiting for you to make a decision. If this is your lifestyle habit, then it will likely damage your relationships.

To overcome this weakness, first accept ownership of your *choice* to be indecisive. Second, establish a *goal* to overcome this weakness. Third, use *affirmations daily* to be reminded of what needs to be done to overcome this weakness. Here are some suggestions:

> *"I make decisions quickly."*
> *"I can be trusted to make a decision quickly."*
> *"Others depend on me to make a quick decision."*
> *"If you want to make an easy job seem mighty hard, just keep putting it off."*

> *"An indecisive man is unstable in all his ways."* (James 1:8 CSB)

RESIST CHANGE

To *resist* change is defined as *to refuse to alter, modify, substitute, deviate, remove, or replace something from that which has been accepted.*

The High "D" (Choleric) | will resist changing their goal unless the alternate method will achieve better, quicker results. They can then change quickly.

The High "I" (Sanguine) | may resist change if it involves interfering with an established relationship or the change may cause embarrassment. They may also resist change if it puts them at a higher risk of failing or it may cause them to look less favorable with others.

The High "S" (Phlegmatic) | is the one that will resist changing most anything. Their nature is for them to remain the same with that which they have accepted, and are comfortable. They resist change for no reason.

The High "C" (Melancholy) | must have a reason to change. They will resist changing until they have been given a reason and time to analyze whether or not the change is, in their estimation, reasonable.

It is legitimate at times to resist making a change. It becomes a weakness if you *routinely* resist most any change. Resisting change may hold up progress, frustrate others and harm relationships.

To overcome this weakness one must first accept ownership of their *choice* to resist change. Second, a *goal* must be established to overcome this weakness. Third, *use affirmations daily* to be reminded of what needs to be done to overcome this weakness. Here are some suggestions:

> *"I will be objective when considering change."*
> *"I choose to embrace change."*
> *"I choose to discuss the need for the change with one I trust."*
> *"I will change for the benefit of others."*
> *"I will carefully consider the need for the change before I resist."*
> *"I do not fear the unknown."*
> *"I will weigh the benefits and rewards of making the change."*
> *"I am willing to expand my comfort zone."*
> *"I will do what is best for the group."*

PROCRASTINATION

To *procrastinate* is defined as *to put off, postpone or delay doing something.* At times, it is necessary to put off doing something, but it becomes a lifestyle problem if one routinely procrastinates.

The High "D" (Choleric) | will procrastinate if the proposed activity does not help them get better, faster results or someone may take advantage of them.

The High "I" (Sanguine) | will procrastinate if the proposed activity may cause them embarrassment or damage a relationship. The greater the risk of failure will increase the possibility the High "I" will put off a proposed activity.

The High "S" (Phlegmatic) | will procrastinate if the proposed activity may cause conflict or a change in their routine. The High "S" by nature does not have a sense of urgency. They may also be waiting for someone to tell them to begin the activity or project.

The High "C" (Melancholy) | will procrastinate if they are not sure of the right and best way to do the proposed activity. They need to know how to do the activity right to avoid making a mistake.

If this is your weakness realize that because you routinely put off doing things you are likely causing hardship on others. Those depending on you are likely disappointed, frustrated and see you as a selfish person that cannot be trusted. Situations usually get worse because you fail to take action. To overcome this weakness first accept ownership of your *choice* to procrastinate. Second, establish a *goal* to overcome this weakness. Third, *use affirmations daily* to be reminded of what needs to be done to overcome this weakness. Here are some suggestions:

"It is like me to do things quickly."
"I do not put things off."
"I choose to complete projects quickly."

"If you want to make an easy job seem hard, just keep putting it off."
(Olin Miller)

"Until you value yourself, you will not value your time.
Until you value your time, you will not do anything with it."
(M. Scott Peck)

"Procrastination is something best put off until tomorrow."
(Gerald Vaughan)

"Only Robinson Crusoe had everything done by Friday."

PERFECTIONISM

To be a *perfectionist* is defined as *a desire for or being displeased with anything that is not perfect or does not meet extremely high personal standards.*

The High "D" (Choleric) | will not usually strive for perfection because of their natural commitment to getting fast results. They can, however, be forceful when insisting that things be done their way.

The High "I" (Sanguine) | will usually not strive for perfection because of their natural need for having fun and enjoying the moment. The

I-C *(Sanguine-Melancholy)* blend, however, can be an exception. They may seek perfection to demonstrate their vast creative ability.

The High "S" *(Phlegmatic)* | will usually not strive for perfection, but they will relentlessly maintain standards that they have accepted and have become a part of their routine.

The High "C" *(Melancholy)* | is the one who will most likely strive to attain perfection personally and in most everything they do.

If this is your weakness, realize that it is not possible to achieve perfection personally or in what you do. Maintaining this belief will continually cause you to feel guilty, disappointed and frustrated. Realize that those with whom you are associated are likely frustrated with your attempt to be perfect. Remember, we live in an imperfect world. Harriet Braiker said, *"Striving for excellence motivates you; striving for perfection is demoralizing."*

To overcome this weakness, you must first accept ownership of your *choice* to be a perfectionist. Second, establish a *goal* to overcome this weakness. Third, *use affirmations daily* to be reminded of what needs to be done to overcome this weakness. Here are some suggestions:

> *"I choose to do the best that I can, and that is enough."*
> *"I will not be critical of myself when I make a mistake."*
> *"I look for good in people."*
> *"I am placing too much importance on trying to be perfect."*
> *"I will learn from my mistakes, and move on with my life."*

Here are some other things you can do to overcome being a perfectionist:

Count the Cost | Draw a line down the middle of a blank sheet of paper creating two columns. On the left side list the *benefits* of being a perfectionist. On the right side list all the *costs* of being a perfectionist (relationships and health). You will find the costs far outweigh the benefits.

Become aware of your self-talk | Identify your unhealthy, all-or-nothing thinking. Substitute your ANTs (Automatic Negative Thoughts) with POTs (Positive Optimistic Thoughts). Ask yourself questions like, *"Is there a more healthy way of thinking?"* or, *"Are things really as bad as I think?"* or, *"Does it really matter if I do not get this perfect?"*

Set time limits on projects | Do not allow *unlimited* time to be spent on a project. When time is up move on to another project, and accept that you have given enough effort on the project.

A few reminders...

"No one is perfect... that's why pencils have erasers."
(Author Unknown)

"A man would do nothing if he waited until he could do it so well that no one could find fault."
(John Newman)

Ring the bells that still can ring
Forget your perfect offering.
There is a crack in everything;
That's how the light gets in.
(Leonard Cohen)

"To escape criticism - do nothing, say nothing, be nothing."
(Elbert Hubbard)

"The most difficult part of attaining perfection is finding something to do for an encore."
(Author Unknown)

"When you aim for perfection, you discover it's a moving target."
(George Fisher)

"Perfectionism is self-abuse of the highest order."
(Anne Schaef)

NEGATIVE THINKING

To think *negatively* means that one has *a tendency to take the most unfavorable view of people and events; seeing the negative in people and events; a failure to find the positive; a pessimistic view of the world.*

The High "D" (Choleric) | when the High "D" demonstrates negative thinking, it is usually directed toward people who fail to live up to *their* high standards of getting results quickly. They will also become negative if someone has taken advantage of them. They value *results* over people.

The High "I" (Sanguine) | when the High "I" demonstrates negative thinking, it is usually directed toward people that have caused embarrassment. They may also become negative if they perceive they have been disrespected. They value their *image* over people.

The High "S" (Phlegmatic) | will demonstrate negative thinking towards those that try to alter their *routine* or way of doing things. They value their *routine* over people.

The High "C" (Melancholy) | when the High "C" demonstrates negative thinking, it is usually directed toward people that have criticized their *work*. Since they analyze everything and have very High standards to do things right, it is easy for the High "C" to criticize others. They value *being right* over people.

If this is your weakness, realize that your tendency to be *pessimistic* repels others and causes them to withdraw from you. Your negative view devalues people and does significant damage to relationships. No one, not even you, can live up to your *high* standards. You are not realistic; you are being degrading and unreasonable.

To overcome this weakness first accept ownership of your *choice* to think negatively. Second, establish a *goal* to overcome this weakness. Third, *use affirmations daily* to be reminded of what needs to be done to overcome this weakness. Here are some suggestions: I am a positive thinker; I see the good in others; I give others the benefit of the doubt; I encourage others.

> *" I am a positive thinker."*
> *"I see the good in others."*
> *"I give others the benefit of the doubt."*
> *" I encourage others."*

"We can complain because rose bushes have thorns, or rejoice because thorn bushes have roses."
(Abraham Lincoln)

"We don't see things as they are; we see them as we are."
(A. Nin)

"If you think you can do a thing or think you can't do a thing, you're right."
(Henry Ford)

"All you can change is yourself, but sometimes that changes everything!"
(Gary W Goldstein)

FEAR OF FAILURE

A *fear of failure* is defined as *an unpleasant, often strong emotion caused by anticipating psychological harm if you fail to accomplish a goal. It includes feeling emotionally overwhelmed with high levels of anxiety and even feeling terrified.*

Physiological responses to fear include a faster heart rate, shallow breathing, headaches, stomachaches, or other physical symptoms that prevent you from trying to accomplish a goal.

When you fail to take action to accomplish a task (goal) it is usually because you have decided that avoiding your fear is more important than accomplishing the task (goal). You fear you will lose what is important to you and that is most often related to your temperament.

The High "D" (Choleric) | does not fear failing. They fear not accomplishing a *goal*, so it motivates them to do all they can to be successful.

The High "I" (Sanguine) | fears that their *image* will be damaged if they fail to accomplish a goal.

The High "S" (Phlegmatic) | fears failure because it may cause conflict or others to be *disappointed* in them.

The High "C" (Melancholy) | fears failing because it may cause them to look *incompetent*.

If this is your weakness, realize that you have allowed your fear to stand between you and the accomplishment of the goal.

To overcome this weakness, first accept ownership of your *choice* to fear failure. Second, establish a *goal* to overcome this weakness. Third, *use affirmations daily* to be reminded of what needs to be done to overcome this weakness. Here are some suggestions:

> *"I do not fear failure."*
> *"My goal is more important than my fear."*
> *"If I fail, I'll try again."*

If you study history, you will find that great inventions were discovered after many failed attempts. Consider Thomas Edison and how many attempts he made to discover a filament that would burn a long time. He said, *"I failed my way to success."* Give more importance to accomplishing your goal than you are giving to your fear of failure. Consider the following:

> *"Our doubts are traitors, and make us lose the good we oft might win, by fearing to attempt."*
> (William Shakespeare)

Abraham Lincoln lost six elections before being elected to office.

Henry Ford went bankrupt five times before succeeding with his automobile company.

When Thomas Edison was a child, he was told by his teacher that he was too stupid to learn anything.

Walt Disney was fired by a newspaper editor because he was told, he lacked creativity.

Einstein did not speak until he was four years old. He was told by his teachers that he would never amount to much and was also advised to drop out of high school.

Michael Jordan was cut from his high school basketball team.

Steven Spielberg applied to USC Cinema School twice and was turned down both times.

Babe Ruth struck out 1,330 times.

SUMMARY

Everyone projects a message that is either *effective* or *ineffective*. You can project the most effective message to others when you stay within your natural temperament tendencies absent of anger, fear and deception. Say what you think, be matter-of-fact, without allowing your emotions to be elevated.

Realize that we all have natural weaknesses based on our temperament blend. Becoming a **better you** is directly related to how *willing* you are to overcome your weaknesses.

Chapter Nine

STEP FIVE: BALANCE

Balance your temperament blend

The fifth step to becoming a **better you** is to choose to balance your natural tendencies with the two temperaments that are the least represented in your blend. Balance is the *key* to being a successful and effective person.

The four temperaments represent *different* ways of approaching people and events. In a given situation, a tendency from a particular temperament may be more efficient and effective than another. The key is to be balanced, flexible, and willing to function in any of the four temperaments when it is appropriate. For example, the High "D" (Choleric) temperament is most likely to overlook careful planning to get quick results, whereas, the High "C" (Melancholy) temperament tends to plan *too* carefully and not be concerned about getting results *quickly*. A balance of both is more *effective*.

To this point, the focus has been on the primary and the secondary temperaments that make up your temperament blend. We are a combination of all four temperaments, but the last two have the least amount of influence on your behavior and the least observed by others. This does not mean that these two are not important. It is the traits of the *third* and *fourth* temperaments that are necessary to incorporate into your behavior to become a more well-balanced person.

TEMPERAMENT BLEND	NEED TENDENCIES OF
D-I *(Choleric-Sanguine)*	"S" *(Phlegmatic)* & "C" *(Melancholy)*
D-S *(Choleric-Phlegmatic)*	"I" *(Sanguine)* & "C" *(Melancholy)*
D-C *(Choleric-Melancholy)*	"I" *(Sanguine)* & "S" *(Phlegmatic)*
I-D *(Sanguine-Choleric)*	"S" *(Phlegmatic)* & "C" *(Melancholy)*
I-S *(Sanguine-Phlegmatic)*	"D" *(Choleric)* & "C" *(Melancholy)*
I-C *(Sanguine-Melancholy)*	"S" *(Phlegmatic)* & "D" *(Choleric)*

TEMPERAMENT BLEND	NEED TENDENCIES OF
S-D *(Phlegmatic-Choleric)*	"I" *(Sanguine)* & "C" *(Melancholy)*
S-I *(Phlegmatic-Sanguine)*	"D" *(Choleric)* & "C" *(Melancholy)*
S-C *(Phlegmatic-Melancholy)*	"D" *(Choleric)* & "I" *(Sanguine)*
C-D *(Melancholy-Choleric)*	"I" *(Sanguine)* & "S" *(Phlegmatic)*
C-I *(Melancholy-Sanguine)*	"D" *(Choleric)* & "S" *(Phlegmatic)*
C-S *(Melancholy-Phlegmatic)*	"I" *(Sanguine)* & "S" *(Phlegmatic)*

I am not saying that you need to *be* the two temperaments that are lacking; I am saying that you need to *do* what the other two temperaments represent. Adding the qualities of the third and fourth temperaments is a *choice* that will enable you to have a balanced approach to dealing with the circumstances of life.

Pick from the following list of characteristics that you feel would complement your temperament blend and is lacking in your behavior. Rate your level of need on a scale of 1 to 10; 1 represents a *low* need, and 10 represents a *high* need.

☐ I need to be more result-oriented   *10 9 8 7 6 5 4 3 2 1*

☐ I need to be more direct   *10 9 8 7 6 5 4 3 2 1*

☐ I need to be more assertive   *10 9 8 7 6 5 4 3 2 1*

☐ I need to be more confident   *10 9 8 7 6 5 4 3 2 1*

☐ I need to be more determined   *10 9 8 7 6 5 4 3 2 1*

☐ I need to be more people-oriented   *10 9 8 7 6 5 4 3 2 1*

☐ I need to be more personable   *10 9 8 7 6 5 4 3 2 1*

☐ I need to be more optimistic   *10 9 8 7 6 5 4 3 2 1*

☐ I need to be more expressive   *10 9 8 7 6 5 4 3 2 1*

☐ I need to be more friendly   *10 9 8 7 6 5 4 3 2 1*

☐ I need to be more service-oriented   *10 9 8 7 6 5 4 3 2 1*

☐ I need to be more consistent   *10 9 8 7 6 5 4 3 2 1*

☐ I need to be more patient   *10 9 8 7 6 5 4 3 2 1*

☐ I need to be more calm   *10 9 8 7 6 5 4 3 2 1*

☐ I need to be more accommodating   *10 9 8 7 6 5 4 3 2 1*

☐ I need to accept sudden change   *10 9 8 7 6 5 4 3 2 1*

☐ I need to be more quality-oriented   10 9 8 7 6 5 4 3 2 1

☐ I need to be more organized   10 9 8 7 6 5 4 3 2 1

☐ I need to be more analytical   10 9 8 7 6 5 4 3 2 1

☐ I need to plan more   10 9 8 7 6 5 4 3 2 1

☐ I need to be more diplomatic   10 9 8 7 6 5 4 3 2 1

1. On a separate sheet of paper, write down the problems that have occurred because of a *lack* of these characteristics in your daily behavior. Be specific and brief.

2. Now write out the *reasons* why you should practice these tendencies. How will it help you to become a more balanced person? Be specific and brief.

3. Write out how you will incorporate these characteristics into your daily behavior. Be specific and brief.

4. State your commitment in affirmations.

AFFIRMATIONS

As mentioned before, the use of affirmations is based on the idea that you become what you *think* about. Using an affirmation enables you to think *often* about the new tendency that you wish to add to your behavior. The more you repeat the affirmation during the day, the more likely you will incorporate it into your daily behavior. Before an affirmation works, you must *decide* that you want the new behavior and that you will work on it daily.

Below, you will find sample affirmations to use that will help you develop a *new* behavior. Write each one on a 3x5 card and keep them with you so you can review them several times during the day.

Affirmations to add *High "D" (Choleric)* tendencies

> I am result-oriented.
> Getting results are important to me.
> Change is a necessary part of life.
> I take action.
> How can I look at this, so it's not a problem?
> What are my options to solve this problem?
> I am matter-of-fact when I speak.
> I give feedback because it is the right thing to do.
> I follow through quickly.

Affirmations to add *High "I" (Sanguine)* tendencies

> I enjoy being around people
> I have a positive outlook on life.
> I encourage others.
> I look for the positive.
> I have a kind tone-of-voice.

Affirmations to add *High "S" (Phlegmatic)* tendencies

> I am service-oriented.
> I am accommodating.
> I control my emotions.
> I am patient and calm.
> I am routine.

Affirmations to add *High "C"* *(Melancholy)* tendencies

I am quality-oriented.
I have a plan.
I pay attention to details.
I am organized.
I treat people with dignity and respect.
I am diplomatic with others.

SUMMARY

To achieve balanced behavior, *decide* to incorporate into your daily behavior the characteristics of the two temperament tendencies that are the least represented. For example, if you are an I-C (Sanguine-Melancholy), you need to practice the traits of the "D" (Choleric) and "S" (Phlegmatic). This means to control your emotions and be "matter-of-fact" when communicating with others, as would the High "D". You would also need to be consistent as a High "S".

Whatever your blend is, work on developing the characteristics of the other two, and you will become a well-balanced and more effective person. The process is aided greatly when you use *affirmations* daily to remind yourself of the behavior you wish to develop.

Chapter Ten

STEP SIX: APPRECIATE

Appreciate the temperament of others

The sixth step to becoming a **better you** is to choose to appreciate the temperament tendencies of others.

THE REASON TO APPRECIATE OTHERS

The word *appreciate* is packed with meaning as seen in the definition by the American Heritage® Dictionary: *"to recognize the quality, significance, or magnitude of, to cherish and have a highly favorable opinion of someone or something, to have high regard based on critical assessment, comparison, and judgment."*

Each person thinks, reasons, and functions out of their temperament blend. It is common for people to look at others with a sense of judgment, and conclude that their way of doing things is better. The differences in temperaments teaches us that there are different approaches to life, but different isn't bad...it's just different. Your way is not necessarily better than another person's way of doing something. The reason for you to *appreciate* others is because *you* want to be appreciated by others. We all need to be understood, accepted, and appreciated, regardless of our weaknesses and different approaches to life. Voltaire, (1694-1778), a French philosopher and author said, *"We are all full of weakness and errors; let us mutually pardon each other our follies - it is the first law of nature."*

APPRECIATE THE DIFFERENCES

If you are thinking of those who are different that annoy you, remember there is a high probability that *you* annoy someone as well. Lots of things irritate and annoy us about others, and temperament issues are among them.

Extroverts complain about introverts, and introverts complain about extroverts. He is too outgoing, or not outgoing enough; she talks too much or she doesn't talk enough; he is too accommodating, or he is not accommodating enough; she is not direct, or she is too direct; she is not detailed, or she is too detailed. You get the idea; we *all* complain about each other which feeds discontent and harms relationships.

Knowing about the four temperaments teaches us that there are four *different* approaches to life. All four approaches are necessary and needed for a society to function successfully. We need the natural leaderships capabilities of the High "D" (Choleric), we need the High "I" (Sanguine) to teach us how to enjoy life, we need the High "S" (Phlegmatic) to show us stability, and we need the High "C" (Melancholy) to show us the benefit of detailed planning.

No one can do all four equally well, so we need to depend on others to do those things for which they are naturally equipped. Choose to appreciate and tolerate the different ways the four temperaments approach life. For example:

The High "D" (Choleric) | is result-oriented, so they need something to fix or build. They need a cause for which to fight. They need activity, adventure and to be in charge.

The High "I" (Sanguine) | is people-oriented, so they need excitement, fun, spontaneity, a variety of activities, and many relationships.

The High "S" (Phlegmatic) | is service-oriented, so they need to be of service to others. They need routine, rest, to be able to accommodate others, sincere appreciation, and no interruption in family time. .

The High "C" (Melancholy) | is quality-oriented, so they need something to analyze. They need information, time to think and a plan. They need privacy, serious conversations, reassurance and feedback.

CONFLICT RESOLUTION

The reason for conflict between people is often a lack of understanding that each have natural tendencies that are different. Remember, different is not bad, just different.

When understanding, acceptance, and appreciation are cultivated, irritations will not occur, and relationships will flourish. It's that simple. Tolerate the temperament differences of those with whom you are associated, even learn to appreciate them.

Your mate's temperament can complement yours *if* you allow it to happen.

For example, if you are a High "I" (Sanguine) and you are married to a High "C" (Melancholy), you can benefit and learn from their ability to organize and plan. If you are committed to balancing your temperament tendencies, you have a model of what you need to do right in front of you. If you are a High "C" (Melancholy) married to a High "I" (Sanguine) then learn from your mate how to talk to people, be spontaneous and have fun. I have seen relationships flourish just because they understood and accepted the temperament differences in each other.

It is easy to find fault, flaws, to point out failures and criticize others. How easy it is to find rocks by walking across any open field. However, it takes considerable effort to find gold.

Accept others where they are, and how they are, without trying to change them to be like you. Show respect for others. To respect holds the idea of, *"to refrain from violating something; to show consideration or thoughtfulness in relation to somebody; to show admiration."* To respect another person's temperament tendencies is to show appreciation.

It takes effort to encourage and build up. It's a mindset, a way of thinking that is a result of a philosophy of life. In Ken Blanchard's book, The One Minute Manager he encourages us to find people doing something right and praise them. Imagine if everyone did that! One never knows where a person is in their life or what they are experiencing. The one you talk to next may be the one who needs you to express encouragement and show your appreciation.

SUMMARY

To become a **better you**, choose to understand and appreciate the temperament differences you see in others.

Chapter Eleven

STEP SEVEN: MODIFY

Modify your temperament blend

T he seventh step to becoming a **better you** is to choose to modify your temperament tendencies to meet the temperament needs of others.

The American Heritage Dictionary's definition of *modify* is, *"to alter."* So, be willing to *alter* your natural temperament approach to relate to others according to their temperament approach. Observe how the other person normally responds to you, because the way people respond to you, is how they want you to respond to them.

HOW TO COMMUNICATE EFFECTIVELY

A person's initial response to you will usually represent one of the four primary temperaments. For example, the High "D" is usually brief, direct and to the point; the High "I" is usually friendly, open, and talkative; the High "S" is usually accommodating and soft spoken; the High "C" is usually cautious and detailed in communication. When you respond to another person in a manner that they understand and appreciate, they will respond more favorably to you. The principle is...

*"If I meet the needs of your temperament
it will increase the possibility
of a favorable response"*

FOR EFFECTIVE COMMUNICATION, GO WITH THE FLOW

1. Observe the person's response; usually, the way people respond to you is how they want you to respond to them.

2. A person's response will represent one of the four temperaments.

3. A person will exhibit one response at a time.

4. The response you see may not be the one they continue to use. Once their initial approach is satisfied, they may shift to a different response representing their second temperament.

5. Use appropriate behavior for each response as suggested in the chart below:

HIGH "D" | CHOLERIC	HIGH "I" | SANGUINE
Be brief, to the point	Be friendly and open
Be direct	Build the relationship
Be confident	Be personal
Give them facts	Be willing to listen
Be result-oriented	Never embarrass them
Be practical	Spend informal time with them
Help them save time	Provide them with details
Be very objective, matter-of-fact	Remind them often
Discuss getting better, faster results	Be open about self and feelings
Tolerate assertive, forceful responses	Tolerate their need to talk

HIGH "S" | PHLEGMATIC	HIGH "C" | MELANCHOLY
Be warm and personal	Be considerate and personal
Show interest in family	Allow time for research
Use visual aids	Give reassurance
Have a slow pace	Give feedback
Never hurry a conversation	Give lots of information
Be in control of your emotions	Listen carefully to their ideas
Be willing to repeat information	Be specific, factual and logical
Avoid asking for sudden change	Discuss what is "right" or "best"
Say you "sincerely" appreciate them	Give specific, detailed, instructions
Tolerate their slow pace	Tolerate their need for accuracy

NOTE: Remember, we all have a combination of two temperaments. This means that a person will have needs from *two* temperaments. For example, if you are communicating with an I-C (Sanguine-Melancholy), they need you to be both lighthearted and detailed in conversation.

To communicate effectively with:

The High "D" (Choleric) | will respond favorable to you if you get to the point quickly. They usually do not like to waste words, or get involved in lengthy conversations (unless they have a good reason).

The High "I" (Sanguine) | will respond favorably to you, if you listen and tell them a story, but not with much detail. Smile and laugh! They usually use a lot of words. They like to talk and tell stories. They tend to lose track of time and enjoy the moment.

The High "S" (Phlegmatic) | will respond favorably to you if you speak softly and are not pushy. They usually do not use a lot of words. They like to listen. They do not like intense, emotional conversations.

The High "C" (Melancholy) | will respond favorably to you, if you speak in specific terms, give them details, and the opportunity to ask questions. They usually do not use a lot of words, and will speak only when they have something to say. They do not like others using general, non-specific terms.

HOW TO APPROPRIATELY MODIFY YOUR TEMPERAMENT

Meet people where they are, and they will respond favorably to you. This requires you to modify, adjust, or alter your natural approach, to meet their temperament needs; speak their temperament language, and they will listen. This also requires you not to be concerned about having your temperament needs met. That is a decision for others to make, so...

> *"Do not focus on what others should*
> *do for you, focus only on what*
> *you should do for others."*

How to communicate with others if you are:

The High "D" (Choleric) | If you are a High "D", this means that you should *not* always be brief, direct and to the point. There may be times when you need to listen patiently to a long, detailed story, or a story being told slowly. Your need is for the person to get to the point, but not everyone has that need. Be patient with people, and alter your need to allow the other person to express themselves *their way*. Respond to people as they respond to you. By so doing you will meet the need of the other person, enhance the relationship and have better communication.

The High "I" (Sanguine) | If you are a High "I", this means that you should *not* always talk. There may be times when you need to be brief, direct and to the point. There may be times when you need to listen more than you talk. Your need is for the person to smile, and have fun in the conversation. Do not take it personally, when others do not smile and laugh when you talk to them. Respond to people as they respond to you. By altering your need, you will meet the need of the other person, enhance the relationship and have better communication.

The High "S" (Phlegmatic) | If you are a High "S", this means that you should *not* always be non-emotional when speaking to others. There may be times when you need to express emotion. There may be times when you need to be brief, direct and to the point. Respond to people as they respond to you. By altering your need, you will meet the need of the other person, enhance the relationship and have better communication.

The High "C" (Melancholy) | If you are a High "C", this means that you should not always be detailed when speaking to others. There may be times when you need to get to the point quickly, without much detail; learn to tell a story without all the detail. Respond to people as they respond to you. By altering your need to tell all the details you will meet the need of the other person, enhance the relationship and have better communication.

If you allow a person to annoy you because their behavioral style is different than yours, realize that you are making a *choice* to be upset. In effect, that person is now in control of your emotions. Make a *better choice* and respond to them instead of *reacting*. For example, if you are speaking to a High "C" and they continue to ask for more detail...give it to them. When the person changes their behavior to a different behavioral style, be flexible and change your response to meet the new *need* being presented.

Remember the following two principles and use them as affirmations. Write them on a 3x5 card and keep them with you to review during the day:

"If I meet the needs of your temperament
it will increase the possibility
of a favorable response."

"Do not focus on what others should
do for you, focus only on what
you should do for others."

SUMMARY

To become a **better you**, choose to modify your temperament needs to allow others to express their temperament needs.

Chapter Twelve

CONCLUSION

Temperament knowledge should never be used to excuse inappropriate or immature behavior. The purpose of knowing your temperament is to identify your natural tendencies so that you may develop a plan to use your strengths, and overcome your weaknesses. In so doing you will become a **better you.**

TOWARD YOURSELF

Recognize that you were born with natural temperament tendencies, and that means you are normal. Your temperament strengths represent what you naturally do well, so develop a plan to use your strengths. Your temperament weaknesses represent things that you do not naturally do well, so develop a plan to overcome the impact of the weaknesses that may be interfering with your effectiveness and success.

Recognize that you have temperament *needs*. These *needs* must be met for you to maintain inner harmony and for you to be at your best.

The goal in developing your natural temperament tendencies is to become a more controlled and balanced person. To accomplish this, you need to *understand* what it means to be your temperament blend; you need to *accept* the temperament tendencies that you were given; you need to become comfortable with yourself and *express* your temperament tendencies; you cannot be you *all* of the time in every situation, so you need to *control* your temperament tendencies; to become the best person you can be, you need to become *balanced* by adding the temperament tendencies that you lack that are represented by the two temperaments you process the least.

TOWARD OTHERS

Realize that people are normal, but approach life differently than you do. Be willing to *appreciate* the temperament tendencies of others. Become skilled at *modifying* your temperament tendencies to meet the temperament needs of others. Communication is not what you *say*, it's what the other person *hears*, so learn to speak *their* temperament language. Do not try to change others to meet your expectations, instead love others, and help them to become a more controlled and balanced person.

SUMMARY

I began this book by saying that I discovered a natural progression in applying the temperament concept to my life. As the steps unfolded, it became clear to me that I was becoming a more *mature,* and well balanced person, because of my study and *application* of the temperament concept.

I have personally benefited greatly because of my exposure, study and application of the temperament concept. If you diligently follow these steps, it will help you maximize your potential, become a more mature, well balanced person, and have a more positive impact on others. My desire in writing this book is to help you become a ***better you.***

About the Author

JOHN T. COCORIS

John T. Cocoris has devoted his life since the early 1970's to developing the temperament model of behavior. John has a B.A. from Tennessee Temple University, a Masters of Theology (Th.M.) from Dallas Theological Seminary, a Masters in Counseling (M.A.) from Amberton University, a Doctorate in Psychology (Psy.D.) from California Coast University. John is a licensed counselor in the state of Texas.

John established Profile Dynamics in the early 1980's to develop and promote the temperament model of behavior for use in business and counseling. He has been a management consultant since 1984 and has worked with a variety of companies giving seminars for training managers and sales people. John has been interviewed on the radio and has been featured numerous times on COPE, a national cable TV talk show.

John has written many books and manuals about the temperament model including: *The Temperament Model of Behavior, Understanding Your Natural Tendencies; The Creative Temperament, The Sanguine-Melancholy (I/C); 7 Steps To A Better You, How To Develop Your Natural Tendencies; Discover Your Child's Temperament, Born With Natural Tendencies; A Therapist's Guide to The Temperament Model of Behavior; How to Supervise Others Using The Temperament Model of Behavior; Effective Selling Using The Temperament Model of Behavior; The DISC II Temperament Assessment; The DISC II Temperament Assessment User Guide; DISC II Library,15 Pattern Series; The DISC 3 Temperament Assessment; The DISC 3 Temperament Assessment User Guide; and 3 Reasons Why Christians Go To Counseling.*

REFERENCES

Adams, Francis, translator. The Genuine Works of Hippocrates. Baltimore: The Williams & Wilkins Company, 1939.

Buss, Arnold H., and Robert Plomin. A Temperament Theory of Personality Development. New York: John Wiley & Sons, 1975.

Chess, Stella, and Alexander, Thomas. Know Your Child. New Your: Basic Books, Inc., Publishers, 1987.

Dobson, James C. Parenting Isn't for Cowards. Waco: Word Books, 1987

Eysenck, H. J. The Biological Basis of Personality. Springfield: Bannerstone House, 1967.

_____. The Structure of Human Personality. London: Methuen & Co. LTD., 1953.

Eysenck, H. J., and Michael W. Eysenck. Personality and Individual Differences. New York: Plenum Press, 1985.

Eysenck, H. J., and Sybil B. G. Eysenck. Personality Structure and Measurement. San Diego: Robert R. Knapp, Publisher, 1969.

Glasser, William. Choice Theory, A New Psychology of Personal Freedom. New York: Harper Perennial, 1999.

Hallesby, Ole. Temperament & The Christian Faith. Minneapolis: Augsburg Publishing House, 1962.

Kant, Immanuel. Anthropology from a Pragmatic Point of View. Translator, Mary J. Gregor., The Hague: Martinus Nijhoff.

Keirsey, David, and Marilyn Bates. Please Understand Me - Character & Temperament Types. Del Mar: Prometeus Nemesis Book Company, 1984.

Marston, William Moulton. Emotions of Normal People. Minneapolis: Persona Press, Inc., 1979.

Merrill, David W., Roger H. Reid Personal Styles & Effective Performance. Pennsylvania: Chilton Book Company, 1981.

LaHaye, Tim. Spirit Controlled Temperament. Whaton: Tyndale House Publishers, 1967.

_____. Understanding the Male Temperament. Old Tappan: Fleming H. Revell Co., 1977.

_____. Your Temperament: Discover its Potential. Wheaton: Tyndale House Publishers, 1984.

_____. Transformed Temperaments. Wheaton: Tyndale House Publishers, 1971.

Siegel, Rudolph E., translator. Galen's System of Physiology and Medicine. New York: S. K., 1970.

www.ingramcontent.com/pod-product-compliance
Lightning Source LLC
Chambersburg PA
CBHW072145020426
42334CB00018B/1889